Cambridge Elements

Elements in Women Theatre Makers
edited by
Elaine Aston
Lancaster University
Melissa Sihra
Trinity College Dublin

FEMINIST IMAGINING IN POLISH AND UKRAINIAN THEATRES

Ewa Bal
Jagiellonian University
Kasia Lech
University of Amsterdam

Shaftesbury Road, Cambridge CB2 8EA, United Kingdom

One Liberty Plaza, 20th Floor, New York, NY 10006, USA

477 Williamstown Road, Port Melbourne, VIC 3207, Australia

314–321, 3rd Floor, Plot 3, Splendor Forum, Jasola District Centre, New Delhi – 110025, India

103 Penang Road, #05–06/07, Visioncrest Commercial, Singapore 238467

Cambridge University Press is part of Cambridge University Press & Assessment, a department of the University of Cambridge.

We share the University's mission to contribute to society through the pursuit of education, learning and research at the highest international levels of excellence.

www.cambridge.org
Information on this title: www.cambridge.org/9781009549516

DOI: 10.1017/9781009549561

© Ewa Bal and Kasia Lech 2025

This publication is in copyright. Subject to statutory exception and to the provisions of relevant collective licensing agreements, no reproduction of any part may take place without the written permission of Cambridge University Press & Assessment.

When citing this work, please include a reference to the DOI 10.1017/9781009549561

First published 2025

A catalogue record for this publication is available from the British Library

ISBN 978-1-009-54951-6 Hardback
ISBN 978-1-009-54952-3 Paperback
ISSN 2634-2391 (online)
ISSN 2634-2383 (print)

Additional resources for this publication at www.cambridge.org/Ewa

Cambridge University Press & Assessment has no responsibility for the persistence or accuracy of URLs for external or third-party internet websites referred to in this publication and does not guarantee that any content on such websites is, or will remain, accurate or appropriate.

For EU product safety concerns, contact us at Calle de José Abascal, 56, 1°, 28003 Madrid, Spain, or email eugpsr@cambridge.org

Feminist Imagining in Polish and Ukrainian Theatres

Elements in Women Theatre Makers

DOI: 10.1017/9781009549561
First published online: August 2025

Ewa Bal
Jagiellonian University

Kasia Lech
University of Amsterdam

Author for correspondence: Ewa Bal, ewa.bal@uj.edu.pl

Abstract: This Element explores how women theatre artists in Ukraine and Poland – separately and together – respond to their dynamically shifting sociopolitical realities after the early 2010s events: the pro-European Maidan Revolution in Ukraine and the traditionalist, anti-European governance in Poland, both of which ignited mass women's protests. Engaging with diverse works – new writing, adaptations of classics, musicals, puppetry, and devised productions – Feminist Imagining features artists that explore the connections between patriarchy-rooted violence, gendered nationalism, women's reproductive rights, and decolonial critique. These underpin their transcultural and intersectional alliances and their proposals for concrete scenarios that redefine the past, present, and future, creating specific feminist imaginaries and epistemologies situated in Central-Eastern Europe. The Element captures the feminist turns in Polish and Ukrainian theatres, highlighting the practices of women artists from the so-called Eastern Europe, whose voices have long been nationally and internationally silenced.

This Element also has a video abstract: www.cambridge.org/EWTM_Bal_abstract

Keywords: Ukrainian theatre, Polish theatre, feminist utopias, politics of care, feminist histories

© Ewa Bal and Kasia Lech 2025

ISBNs: 9781009549516 (HB), 9781009549523 (PB), 9781009549561 (OC)
ISSNs: 2634-2391 (online), 2634-2383 (print)

Contents

1 Introduction   1
   Ewa Bal and Kasia Lech

2 Herstories of Poland's 1989 Transformation   12
   Kasia Lech

3 Women in War Taking the Agency Back   27
   Ewa Bal

4 Feminist Practices of Care and Political
   Agencies of Children   39
   Kasia Lech

5 Alliances and Realistic Cross-Border Utopias   51
   Ewa Bal

6 Final Reflections   64
   Kasia Lech and Ewa Bal

    References   67

1 Introduction

Ewa Bal and Kasia Lech

In recent years, there has been a growing number of studies devoted to understanding the sociopolitical roles of women and gender regimes in Central-Eastern Europe from transnational and cross-border perspectives. These works various enquire after the intersectional marginalisation of 'Eastern European' women, the role of socialist regimes and the Western gaze in shaping discourses on women and gender in Central-Eastern Europe, and also feminist movements and women reclaiming their rightful place in historical, cultural and political contexts.[1]

Feminist Imagining in Polish and Ukrainian Theatres contributes to this field of research by not only moving between theatrical representations of women's struggles in the two countries, but also by exploring theatre's role in staging the interrelatedness of these struggles and forging transcultural alliances that facilitate mutual understandings between nations and people who often have conflicting relationships or do not 'see' each other. The women theatre makers who appear in the Element are those who variously propose cultural and social solutions or scenarios that redefine the past, present, and future, creating feminist imaginaries and epistemologies specific to and situated in Central-Eastern Europe.

1.1 Ukraine and Poland after 1990

Ukraine and Poland share a common historical past and geographical proximity: almost 300 years of territorial commonality and statehood, as well as dependence first on the Russian and then on the Soviet Empire, and, finally, after 1990, the building of state independence. The years 1989 and 1991 – key dates for transforming Poland and Ukraine into free states – could have seen new possibilities for a dialogue between the two countries, their people, and their theatres. However, this did not happen as the transformation processes in Ukraine and Poland had different prerogatives, and the countries experienced different, sometimes conflicting, realities. Poland opted for the closest and fastest possible rapprochement with the Western world, entering NATO in 1999 and the EU in 2004. Meanwhile, in Ukraine, despite the independence supported by 90 per cent of the Ukrainian population who voted in the referendum on the 1st of December 1991, there was no immediate radical break from Russian influence, as the previous Ukrainian political elite had not

---

[1] See for example: Glajar and Radulescu, 2005; Pascall and Kwak, 2005; Zychowicz, 2020; Fábián, Johnson and Lazda, 2021; Kasińska-Metryka and Pałka-Suchojad, 2024; Slavova and Stoilova, 2024.

been replaced (Sribna 2011). And it was only around the early 2010s that the two countries, and especially women theatre artists, started to 'see' each other – an emergent state of mutual recognition that was arrived at through differing sociopolitical processes and events.

In Poland, xenophobic, anti-immigrant, and conservative right-wing nationalist sentiments escalated around 2010. They were mainly expressed in the form of discriminatory policies towards women and ethnic and gender minorities. This escalation began after ninety-six people – predominantly Polish political and military leaders – died in a plane catastrophe in Smoleńsk (Russia). The event unsettled the sense of national security in Poland and was manipulated by the far-right into fearmongering narratives that Poland was, once again in its history, under threat, first from Russia and later from refugees, gender studies, and LGBTQ+ communities. Such discourses made Polish society's profound social and political divisions visible. Building on and deepening these rifts, the ultra-right-wing Law and Justice party won the 2015 presidential and parliamentary elections and governed the country until 2023. During this period, the government endorsed anti-women, patriarchal, and ultra-conservative Catholic ideology, which led to a decrease in protection against domestic violence and further restrictions on women's reproductive rights. This was even though Poland, after 1993, already had one of the most restrictive abortion laws in the world, with abortion illegal except in three situations: severe foetal impairment, a threat to the mother's life or health, and pregnancy resulting from a criminal act. In 2020, the far-right Constitutional Tribunal declared the foetal impairment unconstitutional.

Such restrictions ignited women-led mass protests. First, in 2016, in response to a public discussion about the further outlawing of abortion, women organised Czarne Protesty (Black Protests) using black to symbolise mourning for reproductive rights. In 2020, Ogólnopolski Strajk Kobiet (Nationwide Women's Strike, referencing the 1975 Icelandic women's strike) also made the case for reproductive rights as human rights, writing them into an intersectional and transnational history of struggles for equality. The Polish slogan 'Wypierdalać' (Get the fuck out of here) appeared on a banner during a demonstration in Berlin as 'Wipjerdalatsch' (using 'German' spelling); 'Liberté, égalité, wypierdalajté' (connoting the French revolution's motto) featured on many banners across Poland. The massive and militant dimension of the Women's Strike finally led to the fall of ultra-right power in 2023.

The key caesura for the awakening of a social and feminist consciousness in Ukraine occurred in the years 2013–2014. This was the period when revolution broke out on Kyiv's Maidan (square), now known as the Revolution of Dignity. This was in response to Prime Minister Viktor Yanukovych's decision to cancel the Association Agreement with the European Union, which Ukraine had been working on since 2005, and to sign an Association Agreement with Russia instead. Young people first lead a sit-in strike in Kyiv, which subsequently was quelled by police; it went down in history as the 'Heavenly Sotnia' murders. But similar 'maidans' took place across the country, even in Russian-speaking cities like Donetsk and Kharkiv, where they were brutally repressed. Although Yanukovych eventually stepped down and Ukraine signed an Association Agreement with the EU in 2014, this triggered a ferocious Russian response, culminating in the annexation of Crimea, the secession of the Lugansk and Donetsk regions, and, finally, the full-scale invasion in 2022.

Hence, by 2022, a pessimistic mood prevailed in Ukraine, calling into question the sense of patriotic struggle. At the same time, there were alarming reports from the Donbas Region of the torture and rape of Ukrainian citizens in Russian-backed separatist republics, and the forced Russification of children and kidnappings for ransom. This violence against women and children was thus a harbinger of the rape culture that was fully manifested in Russia's full-scale attack. Many Ukrainians, mainly women and children, were forced to leave the country as early as 2014, often choosing Poland as their place of residence. For women, crossing the border from Ukraine – a country with legal abortion – to Poland meant a restriction of their reproductive rights. Thus, over the last ten years, the issues of patriarchy, violence against women and family breakdown have increased ties between women in Poland and Ukraine. Such bonds were also strengthened by the global #metoo movement that impacted both countries (Kwaśniewska, 2021; Chuzhynova, 2025).[2]

1.2 The Element and Its Premise

Feminist Imagining in Polish and Ukrainian Theatres observes how this process of cross-border solidarity between women is reflected in theatre. We explore the 'feminist imaginings' of women theatre makers from Poland and Ukraine and assess their political potential to assist in the socially progressive transformation of Poland and Ukraine. Doing so, enables us to highlight artists' practices related to intersectional feminism and allyship, areas deeply connected to themes of diversity and intersections between power relations and inequalities (Ahmed, 2012, p. 14).

The term 'intersectionality' – first coined by Kimberlé Crenshaw in relation to combined inequalities against Black women in the United States (1989, pp. 139–140) – is used in the Element to address and reflect on the compounding marginalisation of women from Poland and Ukraine. These relate to their

---

[2] For more, see #НеМовчи (Don't Be Silent) and #46th #MeToo Movement in Ukrainian Theatre at www.cambridge.org/Ewa.

identities as women, as mothers, as young women, as transgender women, as 'Eastern Europeans,' as 'Eastern European' women, and as children. Overall, the Element shows how women artists, by exploring their respective states of intersectional marginalisation, begin to form intersectional alliances with other women and marginalised people.

Such alliances grew out of struggles for justice (Butler, 2015) which involve (1) recognising each other's differences, (2) understanding these differences are rooted in multi-situated experiences of marginalisation, and (3) redressing a mutual lack of knowledge and understanding of each other's differences and positionalities (McIntosh and Hobson, 2013, pp. 2, 14–15; Ghabra and Calafell, 2018, pp. 39–41). In short, these alliances are formed by recognising critical and different non-knowings.

The concept of situated knowing and non-knowings relates to Donna Haraway's 'situated knowledge' and Ewa Bal and Mateusz Chaberski's 'situated knowings' (2021). Haraway discusses knowledge embedded in specific social and cultural positioning and experience (1988, pp. 587–590). Bal and Chaberski focus on knowledge creation processes as inherently situational, contextual, contingent, and emergent (2021, pp. 5–6). Through differently situated knowledge and knowings and difference-underpinned alliances, the women artists discussed in this Element attempt to transform their respective countries past, present, and futures, shifting the existing local, national, and international political imaginaries and geopolitics, including those related to epistemology and knowledge-making. However, to appreciate the radical potential of the works the Element discusses, it is vital to understand the patriarchal structures intrinsic to the national cultural imaginary in both countries and their relationship to the discourses of independence on the one hand and, on the other, the situatedness of the feminist processes, which counterbalance those imaginaries.

1.3 Nationalism and Patriarchy in Ukraine and Poland

The last three years of full-scale Russian-Ukrainian war, and the eight years of the border and hybrid war that preceded it, have updated several national imaginaries and mythologies in the Ukrainian collective imaginary and led to their redefinition in art, literature, and theatre. It is important to remember, however, that Ukraine, as a country struggling with its colonial past, has, for most of its history, and especially during the Romantic period of the nineteenth century, internalised imaginaries of itself created as a result of the dominant gaze of neighbouring countries, including Western Europe, as well as Russia and Poland.[3] As Tamara

---

[3] In the Element, we discuss Ukraine and Poland as having a colonial past. While discourses from the Western and Global South paradigms have traditionally overlooked the colonial histories

Hundorova writes, it was Johan Gottfried Herder who gave Ukraine its proper place in European civilisation by including it in the discourse of Euro-Orientalism. The latter became a practice of Western domination and envisaged the discovery, exploitation, colonisation, and 'civilisation' of the East (Hundorova, 2014, p. 93). The discourse of (Euro)Orientalism thus laid the foundations for the Ukrainian ethno-national identity along with the desire for Europeanisation, to become a modern, civilised nation. An important feature of this discourse was its gendering: the West was perceived as civilised, active, rational, and masculine, while the East appeared nostalgic, mystical, passive, and feminine (ibid.).

In the Ukrainian situation, however, a double feminisation was taking place – simultaneously on the part of the West and on the part of the Russian imperial centre, the latter attributing 'otherness' to Ukraine as the provincial and exotic Malorossia ('Little Russia') (Hundorova, 2014, p. 94). Colonisation by the Russian Empire perpetuated the identification of the Ukrainian periphery with the chaotic and unstable feminised borderlands of the Empire. In Ukrainian Romanticism, most clearly represented by Taras Shevchenko, Ukraine is also clearly feminised and associated with the mother, the woman, or the virgin with the child. The source of masculine strength was located in Kozaccchina (pp. 94–95), a semi-mythologised land, a republic of free people living in the steppes.

Like Hundorova, Katarzyna Glinianowicz also draws attention to the typically Polish colonial view of Ukraine, expressed in the gendered discourse of literature. In nineteenth-century literature, the Polish nobleman is often the 'subject of desire', and the erotically exoticized, wild, and passionate Ukrainian woman is the 'object of seduction'. In the Polish literary imaginary, Ukraine was described as a virgin and a lush nature, a fertile black soil, to be seeded by Polish civilisation processes (Glinianowicz, 2014, p. 164). The male coloniser was to be spurred into action by the passionate Ukrainian woman, depicted as 'black-browed beauty' and 'faithful lover' (p. 165). The civilising mission of Western and Russian imperialism and the libidinous Polish rhetoric on Ukraine form the core of colonial imaginaries that persisted throughout the twentieth century.

For instance, the Soviet propaganda painting from the time of the October Revolution, which encouraged Ukrainians to create an independent republic within the USSR, represented an allegory of Ukraine as a pregnant woman crucified by a Polish Lord. A more recent painting by the contemporary artist Yuri Solomko, entitled *Okhliadova karta Ukraiiny* (*A View Map of Ukraine,*

---

in Central-Eastern Europe, numerous studies have shown otherwise. See Thompson (2000), Korek (2007), Cervinkova (2012), and Huigen and Kołodziejczyk (2023).

2008), depicted a naked woman, trying to cover herself by a sheet that was also a map of Ukraine (*Ukraine*, 2021, p. 176). These victimized and eroticized allegories of Ukraine were also alluded to in the work of Vlada Ralko, *Kyivskii Shchodennyk* (*Kyiv Diaries*, 2013–15) (*Ukraine*, 2021, pp.100–103), depicting a naked, kneeling woman wearing garlands on her head, and facing soldiers of the pro-Russian President Viktor Yanukovych, who quelled demonstrations in Kyiv during the Independence Maidan in 2013 and 2014.

In Ukraine, the critique of these victimised imaginings of Ukrainian women and Ukraine as a country was initially expressed at the intersection of visual arts and performance (Zychowicz, 2020) as exemplified by the feminist collective Femen. Like Pussy Riot in Russia, Femen drew public attention to the objectification and sexualisation of Ukrainian women by intervening in public places and exposing their naked breasts. They wanted to draw public attention to the message written on their bodies: 'Ukraine is not a brothel.' It was a blatant indictment of the behaviour of Western football fans visiting the country during the 2012 European Football Championship, hosted by Poland and Ukraine.

In theatre, a feminist critique of women's situation was slower to take effect: emerged in the aftermath of the EuroMaidan (2014) and accelerated in 2022 given the war with Russia. A young generation of female directors and playwrights began to speak openly and critically about the widespread patriarchal power relations in Ukraine at all levels of cultural management, and about Russia's rape culture as a war tactic and the family crisis of producing war-orphaned children.

To elaborate: women theatre makers have addressed issues ranging from sexual harassment in drama education and theatre, exemplified by Kateryna Peknkova's *Buty maystrom* (*Being a Master*, 2021), to the debilitating conditions of female depression caused by emigration from war zones and having to raise children alone like in the Natalka Blok's *Kriz shkiru* (*Through the Skin*, 2018) and in the Natalka Vorozhbyt's *Zeleni koridory* (*Green Corridors*, 2023). Several plays and performances deal with the rape culture in the eastern Russian-occupied territories of Ukraine (see Section 3), as well as with the realities of eastern Ukraine, which is riddled with corruption and materially underfunded like in the Lena Lagushonkova's *Mij prapor zapisal kotyk* (*Kitten Peed on my Banner*, 2022) and *Shchodennyk Donbasu* (*Donbas Diaries,* 2020). Finally, after the outbreak of full-scale war, the theatre responded to the initial shock of what was happening (Nina Zakhozhenko, *Ja norm/I'm ok.* 2022).[4] Although many plays responding to the onset of war were not performed in the repertoires of leading theatres, they did find a place in studio and fringe stages

---

[4] For further examples see: https://ukrdrama.ui.org.ua/ (30.01.2025); https://ukrdramahub.org.ua/collection/bez-nykh (30.01.2025); https://kurbas.org.ua/news/nenazvana-viuna/nenazvana-viuna.html (30.01.2025).

like Teatr Dramaturkhiv (The Playwrights Theatre) in Kyiv, Jam Factory Art Center and Lesia Ukrainka Academic Theatre in Lviv. Most importantly, these works were translated into many foreign languages and staged abroad, thus increasing the resonance and international profile of Ukrainian women playwrights.

Furthermore, the generation of female directors to emerge post 2014 frequently practised their craft in dialogue with Polish theatre makers. Some of the most remarkable collaborations were the Polish workshops 'Director – Playwright – Dramaturge: Formation of an Idea' organized in partnership with the Ukrainian NGO 'Theatre Platform' (2014); and 'Theatre Desant' in partnership with the NGO 'Drabyna' (2015–2016). Other initiatives were oriented towards the realisation of productions, such as *Mapy strachu mapy indentychnosti* (*Maps of Fear – Maps of Identity*, 2016) and *Mij did' kopal, mij bat'ko kopal, a ja ne bydu* (*My dad used to dig, my father used to dig, and I won't*, 2018), both about the biographies of young people from the Donetsk and Luhansk regions, and produced by Joanna Wichowska together with the Ukrainian director Roza Sarkisian. Another Ukrainian female director Olena Apchel (now an enrolled soldier in the Ukrainian Army) created at least two productions in Polish theatres: *Więzi* (*The Ties*, 2019) at the Wybrzeże Theatre in Gdańsk (about the fate of a woman subjected to internal and external emigration) and *Kreszany* (*The Trees' Spirits*, 2021) in Zagłębie Theatre in Poland (a feminist war manifesto and expression of nostalgia for the lost homeland in Donbas). There were also Katarzyna Szyngiera's and Przemysław Wlekły's two projects: *Swarka* (*A Fight*, Bydgoszcz, 2015), *Lwów nie oddamy* (*Lviv, we won't give it up!*, Rzeszów, 2018), which explored mutual Polish-Ukrainian relations of the borderland.

The gendered imaginaries and their contemporary rethinking in Ukraine resonate with dominant discourses in Poland. As Maria Janion pinpoints, 'Polish national culture is remarkably masculine' (2006, p. 266). She refers here to the national imagining of Poland and its community, which culture in general – and theatre in particular – has facilitated since Poland first lost its independence in 1795 to Russia, Prussia (later Germany), and Austria. In the Romantic period, Polish male playwriting gained enormous power to shape discourses related to Poland. This Romantic paradigm – as we will refer to it throughout the Element – dominated the national liberation narratives and identity projects throughout the nineteenth and twentieth centuries. They were absorbed into the patriarchal discourse of Poland's transformation, legitimising the exclusion of women as a pernicious feature of Polish early democracy (Graff, 1999; Kościelniak, 2018, 2024). The artists in this Element are in direct dialogue with the Romantic paradigm, particularly challenging how it imagined Polish women, the Polish community, and its relationship with the 'Other.'

For a start, Romantics tied Polish identity to Catholicism and to the core ideas, which defined Polish male martyrology: messianism, and Prometheism. The former was based on the conviction that the Polish nation had been chosen by God to be sacrificed for the freedom of the world, similar to how Jesus Christ was sacrificed to redeem humanity. Prometheism, based on the Prometheus myth, expressed the necessity of individual sacrifice for the freedom of all humankind – or, in the Polish case, the nation – and the ability of the individual to rebel against God, who abandoned Poland. The artistic interpretation of Polish male martyrology is evinced in the Romantic play *Dziady* (*Forefathers' Eve*) by Adam Mickiewicz, the text which many artists in this Element are in a critical dialogue with. This is because *Dziady*, in many ways, defined Polish theatre, its relationship to society, and the Polish community, mobilising its 'performative creation' (Kosiński, 2010, pp. 117, 122) that was deeply gendered.

Dziady, through its main character – the poet-lover Gustaw transformed into the national hero Konrad – dramatised and affirmed the sense of national solidarity based on homosocial brotherhood enabled by idealised (and desexualised, apart from the reproductive function) motherhood (Ostrowska, 2004, pp. 216–219; Janoszka, 2014). Romantics saw enslaved Poland as the mother of all Poles, sanctified by the status of Holy Mary as the Queen of Poland and mother of Poles, rooted in the Middle Ages. This conception of motherhood embodied by the figure of Matka Polka (Polish Mother) is glorified in *Dziady* and Mickiewicz's poem *Do Matki Polki* (*To the Polish Mother*) that accompanied the play.

Polish Mother was at the heart of national liberation ideas: she passed on Polish spiritual and physical heritage to new generations of Poles. Her sacred duty was to give birth, feed with breastmilk made of her blood and raise sons so that they might die for Poland's freedom, just as Mary raised Jesus to die for humanity. In doing so, she was sanctifying the 'blood and milk' oath that created the nation as a homosocial brotherhood (Janoszka, 2014). In *Dziady*, this was dramatised in the so-called 'Vengeance Song', which Konrad sang with a brotherhood of (male) prisoners, announcing the necessity of drinking the enemy's blood to free Poland.[5]

---

[5] Our historization contextualises the dominant socio-political-cultural models relevant to the artists featured in this Element. We thus do not explain the complex and ambiguous discussions surrounding women's emancipation and patriarchy in the Interwar and post-WWII periods. For those interested in the topic, English-language resources include Strokata, 1980; Hrycak, 2001; Żarnowska, 2004; Fidelis, 2010; Fidelis et al., 2014.

Dziady also exemplifies how Polish Romantics laid the foundations for post-transformation understandings of motherhood in patriarchal and feminist contexts as either a woman's sanctified fate or a fate from which women should be defended. The former has already been explained. The latter related to the banning of abortion in 1993, which – together with motherhood politicised by Romantic, patriarchal and Catholic discourses – created circumstances in which Poland's feminist movement in the 1990s initially saw motherhood and women's rights as antagonistic (Graff, 2014b, pp. 31–33).

The harbinger of change was Antonina Grzegorzewska and Anna Augustynowicz's 2010 *Migrena* (*Migraine*) presented in Szczecin's Współczesny Theatre. Taking ecofeminist perspective, it explored how patriarchal discourses on motherhood enabled sexual violence and violence against women, children, and animals. However, only around 2014, mainly due to Agnieszka Graff's book *Matka Feministka* (*Mother Feminist*), did motherhood start to be discussed as a feminist issue. Around the same time, Polish feminism started abandoning the idea of feminism as a homogeneous and united movement. It began appreciating differences and disputes as core features of Polish feminism and engaged with issues previously excluded from feminist discussions, such as social class structures, children and religion (Graff, 2014a). This is important as the paradigm of the gender binary, sanctified by the Catholic Church (Kościelniak, 2018, 2024), also impacted other groups. Within such a paradigm, there was no possibility to recognise the right to marry single-sex couples, the psychiatric problems of young people associated with homophobia and transphobia, or the agency of children.

Theatre engaged with these debates and became their critical partner. Increasingly, artists staged women's voices and perspectives, interrogating the Romantic paradigm, nationalistic discourses, patriarchal power structures, and the relationship between Poland and the Catholic Church.[6] Several projects focused on Polish women forgotten by history, including theatre history. Since 2012, a collective of women has run HyPaTia, a research project rediscovering Herstories of Polish theatre.[7] More and more open criticism of the Catholic Church emerged, most spectacularly perhaps in 2017 *Klątwa* (*The Curse*), directed by Olivier Frljić (Warsaw), in which abortion was discussed, crosses were turned into rifles, and one of the actors performed fellatio on a sculpture of John Paul II. *Klątwa* – based on the 1899 text by Stanisław Wyspiański – also exemplifies how adaptations of the classical repertoire acted as a critical lens

---

[6] This is not to say that Polish theatre was not critically engaging with socio-political realities before. It was (see for example Lease, 2016), but we want to show the increased interest in particular themes.

[7] See: www.hypatia.pl/ (30.01.2025).

towards marginalisation, in this case, of women. Radosław Rychcik's *Dziady* (Poznań, 2016) and Augustynowicz's *Burza* (*The Tempest*) (Szczecin, 2016) asked questions about exclusion empowered by Polish male martyrology, racism, and ableism.

Seeking to change such marginalising practices became a reason for founding theatres such as Warsaw's feminist Theatre Poliż and disability-led Centrum Sztuki Włączającej/Teatr 21 (Centre for Inclusive Arts/Theatre 21). Theatre for young audiences, various pedagogic and care-led projects in Polish theatre increasingly began to explore urgent political questions, filling, or at least addressing, the gaps in state officialdom and provision. Maria Wojtyszko and Jakub Krofta, in their puppetry *Sam, Czyli Przygotowanie Do Życia w Rodzinie* (*Sam, Or Preparation For Family Life*, Wrocław, 2014), explored how children were systemically abandoned by welfare institutions. *Edukacja seksualna* (*Sexual Education*) by Michał Buszewicz (Szczecin, 2022) talked about sexuality and coming-of-age, which Polish schools did not provide. In Jakub Skrzywanek's *Spartakus. Miłość w czasach zarazy* (*Spartakus. Love in the time of Cholera*, Szczecin, 2022) one-sex couples could get married on stage.

1.4 Structure and Methods

The historical, sociopolitical, and cultural backgrounds explained here situate our questions about the 'feminist imaginings' in Ukraine's and Poland's theatres, demonstrating the multiplicity of perspectives from which these questions could be tackled. We chose to pursue them through contexts which highlight: (1) how Ukrainian and Polish women interrogate oppressive patriarchal structures underpinned by Romantic imaginaries, struggles for independence, and religion, (2) how they challenge the positioning of women and other marginalised groups facilitated by these oppressive structures, (3) processes of Polish and Ukrainian women's voices coming together, and (4) the political potential of their transnational alliances.

We look first at how women rediscover their histories and political agencies over the past and present in national contexts. In Section 2, Kasia Lech examines various works that propose gender, sexuality, age, and intersectionality as critical categories for retelling and understanding the transformation and its consequences for Poland's society. Plays considered in this section demonstrate feminist interrogations of collective memories and the rediscovery of diverse women's voices and their leadership of political events that saw the fall of communism in 1989. Overall, they reveal multiple Herstories of transformation and showcase their political potential to rethink human-to-human relations in Poland.

In Section 3, Ewa Bal shows how, in the realities of war, Ukrainian theatre creates awareness of the disintegration of cultural patterns associated with masculinity and femininity and diagnoses the far-reaching effects of rape culture as a war tactic of the aggressor. At the same time, using the concept of cracking the field of recognition (Butler, 2015, Bal, 2023b), Bal evidences how the artistic strategies of Ukrainian women artists dismantle the epistemic foundations of the patriarchal world by incorporating feminist strategies of resistance.

Thereafter, discussion focuses on the feminist imagining of alternative ways of living and relating in-between societies. The fourth section by Lech explores theatre for young children as a site of urgent feminist imagining and action underpinned by the politics of care. Focusing on theatre made in the context of the 2015 humanitarian crisis, the global COVID pandemic, and the 2022 full escalation of the Russian invasion of Ukraine, the discussion shows how alliances between women and children foster mutual empowerment and make it possible to imagine more hopeful futures.

The final section by Bal reflects on the theatre projects created within the framework of Polish-Ukrainian artistic alliances, understood as difficult and unpredictable pacts made in the name of the struggle for social, political and economic justice. By analysing the affirmative projects of the future that emerge from these alliances, Polish-Ukrainian theatres propose alternatives to Romantic models of patriotism and gendered social roles, replace the patriarchal Greco-Judeo-Christian tradition with feminist Slavic mythologies, and show future worlds in which no church, especially the Catholic Church, plays a leading role. At the end of this section, we offer a jointly authored, concluding summary that highlights the Element's key findings and insights on 'feminist imagining' in Ukraine's and Poland's theatres.

Across all the sections, we cover diverse socio-geographical landscapes, paying attention to works created in large cultural centres such as Kyiv, Kharkiv, Lviv, Wrocław, or Warsaw, as well as less-known cities such as Sosnowiec, Szczecin, Donieck, or Luhansk. We also provide links to selected trailers and fragments of productions we discuss (in footnotes) and offer linguistic access to fragments from Ukrainian and Polish artistic and scholarly texts. Unless stated differently, all these translations were by Lech (Sections 2 and 4) or Bal (Sections 3 and 5).

This introduction, as well as the Element overall, reflects shifting, differing and destabilising contexts, transnational dialogues and alliances. The same obtains for the Element's language, our situatedness as authors and the process of writing. We purposely do not unify our different writing styles, and when referring to Ukraine and Poland, we constantly change the order. This links with how our lived experiences of migration emphasise for us that we are both at home and not-at-home in the theatres about which we write. Bal – who authors Element's sections about Ukrainian and Ukrainian-Polish productions – is an expert in Ukrainian theatre in Poland, her country of origin and now residence. Her expertise is recognised in Ukraine, where she often works in the Ukrainian language. Lech is a Polish-born and trained actor, but she has lived abroad for the last twenty years. At the same time, she visits Poland at least quarterly, regularly writes about Polish theatre, and is involved in Polish research projects. In short, our positions challenge national boundaries and are ambiguous. On the one hand, they allow for a critical migratory gaze; we perceive the contexts that we analyse as simultaneously familiar and unfamiliar, which reveal different layers and complexities. On the other hand, we have an enhanced sense of our not-knowings, and an enhanced need for dialogues and alliances.

In writing this Element, we were each other's allies. We remained in daily contact over the phone and emails, we read out-loud fragments of our texts to each other, and we were mutual peer-reviewers. We wrote the Introduction and the summary together, both synchronously and asynchronously. We shared folders, documents, ideas, and contacts. We challenged each other's interpretations. We accommodated our very different body clocks and schedules. All this while travelling across three languages (Ukrainian, Polish, English). But, at the same time, we were not enough. This Element grew on emotions and reflections provided by conversations, meetings, and performances that we shared with artists, activists, curators, and scholars from Ukraine and Poland. Through these conversations, festival visits, engaging with live and recorded theatre, and reading local theatre criticism and scholarship, we were constantly in dialogue with differently situated local perspectives. Some of these voices are present in the references and bibliography. We thank them all at the end of the Element.

2 Herstories of Poland's 1989 Transformation

Kasia Lech

What happens to Polish historical narratives and collective memories if one approaches them assuming that women *are* humans and their stories and perspectives matter? This is a question which Agnieszka Graff ironizes in her preface to Marcin Kościelniak's *Aborcja i demokracja* (*Abortion and democracy*) (Graff, 2024, p. 14). In this monograph, Kościelniak shows that the 1945–1989 process towards Poland's freedom was, in fact, a process towards men, the state, and the Church gaining control over women. From the perspective of women's rights, he argues, the 'peaceful' transformation from the communist state into a democracy was a history of Polish women losing their freedom, as manifested in the 1993 anti-abortion law (Kościelniak, 2024). They also lost their place in the history of Poland's freedom. While women played critical political and social roles in the fall of communism, such events have long been narrated and remembered in Poland and abroad as constitutive of a male revolution.

Section 2 focuses on women artists' responses to the 1989 Polish transformation and their performances of its Herstories from increasingly multivocal and intersectional perspectives. The featured works, directly and indirectly, pre-echo Kościelniak's aforementioned diagnosis and his interest in gender as an essential category for historical analysis. Kościelniak refers to Joan Wallach Scott's arguments for gender as 'a primary field within which or by means of which power is articulated' and as a 'persistent and recurrent way' to allow the manifestation of power to happen (Scott, 1988, pp. 44–45; Kościelniak, 2024, pp. 19, 32). I will discuss theatre works that speak to Scott's points, situating them in Poland's collective memory of transformation and in relation to the women it forgot. The artists propose sexuality, age, and intersectionality as other critical categories for understanding 1989 and its consequences for Poland's society. These categories allow for examinations of social relations, revealing the stories of different women and, through that, interconnections between power structures and marginalisations of other identities. Thus, they pave the way for a deeper understanding of inequalities, discrimination, and oppression in contemporary Poland (Mintz, 2008; Wiesner-Hanks, 2015; Díez-Bedmar, 2022; Kuefler, 2024).

2.1 Polish Transformation and Forgotten Women

The fall of communism in Poland and the Soviet Block is inherently connected with Solidarność as the Block's first officially recognised trade union, which grew into a social and political movement. Solidarność was founded in August 1980 as the outcome of the strikes in the Gdańsk shipyard. The initial reason was the firing of crane operator Anna Walentynowicz and electrician Lech Wałęsa, but also food shortages in Poland. After the authorities accepted the first demands, the protesters were about to stop the strikes. However, a series of interrelated events saw not a cessation but an escalation of strike action.

For a start, tram driver Henryka Krzywonos stopped the tram at the Baltic Opera building, symbolically announcing the Gdańsk public transport staff joining the shipyard strike, which, in turn, immobilised the city. Instrumental in spreading the strikes was also Alina Pienkowska, who managed to communicate the news about the Gdańsk events to another opposition leader, Jacek Kuroń. He, in turn, communicated it further, including to the international press.

Moreover, after Wałęsa wanted to end the strike, a group of women – including Walentynowicz, Pienkowska, Krzywonos, and Ewa Ossowska – stopped the protesters from leaving the shipyard. Soon, workers in over 700 establishments all over Poland – including shipyards, mines, universities, theatres, and factories – joined the strikes. As a result, the so-called August agreements – co-developed by women and now included in the UNESCO World's Documentary Heritage – were signed. They included the right to trade unions, strikes, free speech, increased childcare places, and three-year paid maternity leave. Solidarność was officially registered in November 1980 as Niezależny Samorządny Związek Zawodowy (Independent Self-Governing Trade Union) Solidarność, with membership that soon reached ten million. Approximately half of the members were women.

The August agreements created a short period of relative liberation and democratisation of some parts of social life, for example, through the loosening of censorship laws, that allowed independent media to develop. However, on 13 December 1981, General Wojciech Jaruzelski – then Poland's communist leader – announced a state of emergency and introduced martial law, which put the country under military rule until 1983. Many women and men connected to Solidarność were arrested. Despite this, Solidarność survived underground. In 1983, the Nobel Peace Prize was awarded to Lech Wałęsa for his contribution to human rights. His wife, Danuta Wałęsa, received it on his behalf because of fears that the communist regime would not allow Lech back into the country.

Empowered by this and by the social and international support, Solidarność grew into a movement that ultimately led to the 1989 Round Table Talks, in which Solidarność and the government agreed to form a bicameral parliament, an institution of a president, and to hold a semi-free election in which 65 per cent seats in the lower chamber was guaranteed to the communist party. The election happened on 4 June 1989. The democratic opposition won 161 out of 161 seats possible in the lower chamber and 99 (out of 100) in the higher chamber. A Solidarność-led government was formed. This was the symbolic end of communism in Poland and the start of the country's road to democracy. In 1990, Lech Wałęsa was elected as the President of Poland.[8]

This brief outline signals the critical role of women, their multi-layered leadership, during the 1980s political crises in Poland. However, the collective memory of the events – in Poland and abroad – has been dominated by images and stories of men: Lech Wałęsa's jump over the fence of the Gdańsk shipyard; Wałęsa's signing of the August agreements with a large red pen with an image of

---

[8] The current section refers to these decade-long developments as the 1989 events or the transformation.

Pope John Paul II; Jacek Kuroń's articles about the reforms needed to the country and to socialism, and his repeated arrests; Władysław Frasyniuk's legendary escape from the communist authorities during the martial law and his leadership of the Solidarność underground. The Round Table Talks have been discursively constructed as a socially led and peaceful transformation; there is no mention of how, at the decisive meetings, out of fifty-eight people present, only two were women: Anna Przecławska (representing the communist government) and Grażyna Staniszewska (representing the opposition). The Catholic Church had three official representatives.

American scholar Shana Penn interrogated the representation of the transformation in Poland and abroad and rediscovered histories of women (1994, 2005). Penn deconstructed the myth of 1989 as a male revolution. Exploring the institutionalised invisibility of women in the transformation histories, she showcased vital roles that women played in the events. She also analysed the complex reasons behind the invisibility, including Poland's local politics, Poland's traditions connected to Romanticism and the national-liberation movement, the Catholic Church, the secrecy of some anti-communist actions, the male gaze, the Western gaze which perceived the events through its ideas on freedom and feminism, and the institutionalised and 'culturally encoded agreement' of women to remain invisible (Penn, 2005, pp. 14–18). It took theatre much longer to notice the women of Solidarność and to offer a feminist analysis of the events. The pioneers of the 1989 Herstories were works by Julia Holewińska, Paweł Palcat, and Krystyna Janda.

2.2 Understanding Poland's Transformation through the Multiplicity of Women's Experiences

Julia Holewińska's *Ciała Obce* (*Foreign Bodies*) won the 2010 Gdynia Drama Award, the most prestigious prize for new Polish plays and was first staged in 2012 by the Wybrzeże Theatre in Gdańsk. *Ciała Obce* was inspired by Ewa Hołuszko's biography, a transgender woman and an important member of the Solidarność movement. The play offered a critical feminist engagement with Poland's historiography connected to the transformation. It also pre-figured Kościelniak's proposal to read Poland's fight for independence from the perspective of women's rights as a (hi)story 'about the transition from freedom to the systemic violence of the non-secular state' (Kościelniak, 2024, pp. 32–24). Holewińska's play did precisely that.

Ciała Obce interrogated the gender binary and its consequences for Poland's society, history, and collective memory. The main character in *Ciała Obce* is Adam, presented as one of the Solidarność's heroes, who, after 1989, undergoes a sex reassignment procedure to become Ewa. As a woman, Ewa is written out of history. Her family – including her son – and her friends distance themselves from her; she is rejected by the Catholic Church and 'forgotten' by her fellow Solidarność members. The fragmented and non-linear structure emphasised how gender binarism determined Adam's and Ewa's stories: the scenes happening in pre-1989 Poland and post-1989 Poland alternated, and the gender of the main character indicated the time. Hence, the play highlighted the contrast between the protagonist when perceived as a man and when as a transgender woman, arguing for the social acceptance of Ewa as a woman and as a transgender person.

To situate Ewa's marginalisation in the broader context of gendered Poland's histories, Holewińska played with form and intertextuality. The Female and Male Chorus commented – often in rhymed prose – on scenes and characters referencing language and gender roles that the Romantic paradigm, Polish national liberation movement, and the Catholic Church had created and resolutely endorsed. The characters were named to recall figures from Polish history and culture associated with the national liberation myths and movement, and Holewińska emphasised these links in her stage directions. Adam/Ewa's son was Lech, like the legendary founder of Poland and Lech Wałęsa as the 'legendary saviour' of Poland from communism. One of their friends was Jadwiga, recalling a teenage queen of Poland glorified in national memory for being sacrificed and married to a much older man to save Poland. Adam's wife was Maryjka, from Maryja, the mother of Jesus and, in the national liberation tradition, the mother of Poles. The multiple references to Adam Mickiewicz's *Dziady* (*Forefather's Eve*) deepened the dialogue with the Romantic paradigm and patriarchal national traditions but also emphasised the contrast with how the characters' transformations radically differed in each of the two plays. In *Dziady*, the transformation of Romantic lover Gustaw into Romantic warrior Konrad ensured Konrad's status as a model national hero for centuries; in *Ciała Obce*, the transformation of Adam into Ewa wrote Ewa out of history and society.

To exemplify, consider this scene that dealt with motherhood as an embodiment of the symbolic presence and actual absence of women in Poland's collective memory. It started with a Male Chorus recalling images of mothers in Polish culture and history. This included mothers as tender and caring figures, 'Polish Mother', and different religious and Romantic images of Mary as a mother of Jesus and Poland. This framed the scene in which Adam and Maryjka confronted each other's ideas on motherhood. Maryjka wanted a life outside of motherhood and refused to breastfeed; Adam dreamt about being a breastfeeding mother. Adam resented Maryjka's views, and she resented his, which play made apparent later when Ewa was alone and when her son told her that Ewa's gender reassignment was the reason for Maryjka's death. The accusation framed Ewa's gender reassignment as a deadly sin against society, the country, and the religion: she killed her wife and, symbolically, the mother of Poland and Jesus. This was also enhanced by her name – 'Ewa' in English is Eve – which referenced the woman cast in the patriarchal reading of the Bible as humankind's first sinner.

Holewińska's presentation of the characters in relation to broader, social structures critiqued the multiple co-existing axes of oppression – communism, gender binarism, Romantic paradigm, Poland's national-liberation movement, and the Catholic Church – that imprisoned the characters, even though some of these were seen as auguring freedom. By extension, *Ciała Obce* interrogated not only the gender binary but also the dichotomy between pre- and post-1989 Poland as 'imprisoned' and 'free,' questioning the idea of freedom and to whom it was given.

While Holewińska's play engaged with gender to critically interrogate the transformation, other early works made the case for women's stories as essential for understanding the 1989 events. In March 2011, *Zrozumieć H. (Understanding H.)* – written and directed by Paweł Palcat – was presented at the Song Interpretation Contest in Wrocław and later included in the repertoire of the Modjeska Theatre in Legnica. *Zrozumieć H.* re-read the history of transformation through the biography of Henryka Krzywonos. In *Zrozumieć H.*, the fragmented storytelling, enhanced by the tension between the dramatic time (thirty years) and the time of the performance (approximately sixty minutes), worked against ideas of linear and stable history and memory. This was also because Henryka was performed by three actors, all in their twenties: Magda Skiba, Zuza Motorniuk, and Ewa Galusińska.

The production mixed documentary recordings of the transformation events with scenes that presented fragments from Krzywonos' life and her various protests. She was shown as a child growing up in a precarious context, standing up to her violent father, as a woman tram driver who takes a leadership role in the Solidarność strikes, and a woman who made a conscious choice to abandon her political career and become an adoptive mother in a family foster home. All her choices were framed as heroic acts that resisted society's expectations of her as a woman. On the one hand, this interrogated the idea of a (male) hero and, on the other, showed how stories and agencies of women, including little girls and mothers, are interwoven in Poland's fight for independence. At different levels, *Zrozumieć H.* incorporated the perspectives of children as an important part of the historical and political narratives, questioning patriarchal notions of children and their memories as untrustworthy narrators. Henryka's story as a little girl is an essential part of the production, which was created by theatre makers who experienced the transformation events as young children.

Stagings of the 1989 Herstories also sometimes took the form of a one-woman show. The most famous of these was the 2012 production *Danuta W.* based on Danuta Wałęsa's autobiography *Marzenia i tajemnice* (*Dreams and secrets*). Katarzyna Kułakowska and Agata Łuksza read Wałęsa's autobiography as one of the signs of the 'feminine turn' in Polish historical narratives and the first moment in which a critical perspective of 'Polish Mother has been heard and heeded' (2015, pp. 55, 62). In the book – a bestseller in Poland – Wałęsa narrated the events leading up to and post-1989 from the perspective of a woman fighting for her family to survive as a Polish woman.[9] She reflected on her growing awareness of her marginalised position as a woman from communist Poland – a woman with a primary education who was raised in the countryside in a Catholic family who taught her to serve her husband. But she reclaimed her agency: broke her public image of a quiet Catholic wife and mother, spoke critically about her husband and the Catholic Church.

The iconic Polish actress – culturally associated with anti-communist opposition – Krystyna Janda adapted *Marzenia i tajemnice* and performed it as *Danuta W*, reading the book as a history of Poland as seen by a woman and, specifically, by Danuta Wałęsa.[10] To emphasise such a reading, Janda did not embody Wałęsa but acted as Janda, a female performer and Janda, a Polish woman citizen performing Polish (hi)stories. Janda's production – directed by Janusz Zaorski – premiered in October 2012 at the Wybrzeże Theatre in Gdańsk with Danuta and Lech Wałęsa present. Kułakowska and Łuksza say that Janda's work extended and supported the processes of including women's voices in the discourses on Solidarność and transformation (2015, p. 65).

A more recent contribution to staging the Solidarność Herstories came from Anna Gryszkówna and Agnieszka Przepiórska. In 2023, at the Nowa Łaźnia Theatre in Kraków, they premiered *Nazywam się Anna Walentynowicz* (*My name is Anna Walentynowicz*). Based on a biography written by Dorota Karaś and Marek Sterlingow, and adapted by Piotr Rowicki, this one-woman show was performed by Przepiórska as Anna Walentynowicz, exploring her journey from a young girl who had to work since she was twelve, through a woman welder who believed in communism, to the woman crane worker who led the fight against it.

Children's perspectives on Poland's past – rendered in *My name Is Anna Walentynowicz* and in *Zrozumieć H.* – were crucial to another of Holewińska's

---

[9] Katarzyna Kułakowska and Agata Łuksza explore the phenomenon of Wałęsa's book in detail; their article is of interest to those wanting to know more (2015).

[10] For the trailer see: www.youtube.com/watch?v=pMkO9PKKpj4.

plays, the 2011 *Rewolucja Balonowa* (*Bubble Revolution*). This made an argument for children's memories as crucial historical material and showed age allied to gender as a valid category for historical and political analysis. *Rewolucja Balonowa* was written as a manifesto of Poles born in the 1980s. In the play, their voices were embodied by Wiktoria, who narrated the events between the 1980s and 2000s, looking at Poland during communism, Solidarność, the early democracy, and until it became a member state of the European Union. The latter – combined with the economic crisis – evoked a mass migration of those born in the 1980s to other EU countries (Krings *et al.*, 2013, p. 41; Okólski and Salt, 2014, p. 18).

In the play, Wiktoria reflects on a sense of abandonment by her parents – preoccupied with the political and economic aspects of the transformation – and her disappointment with the freedom that did not meet the expectations created by colourful magazines, American soap operas, and later by the promise of equality and prosperity as a member of the European Union. As a child, she talked about food shortages, which, for her, manifested in the lack of sweets available to the daughter of her father's superior. As a teenager, she speaks about the simultaneous sexualisation of women on television and in advertisements and the lack of conversation or spaces for her as a young woman to learn about sex. The end of censorship, together with capitalism, brought about the mass sexualisation of society and, with that, the sexualisation of Polish women's bodies, as shown by researcher Ewa Stusińska. However, partly due to the growing presence and control of the Catholic Church over the public sphere, there was no space to develop positive approaches to sexuality (Stusińska, 2021). In *Rewolucja Balonowa*, Wiktoria gets pregnant after having sex for the first time, and since abortion is banned, she has no choice but to have a baby. In other words, through her childhood and coming-of-age memories, Wiktoria critically comments on political events, social hierarchies pre- and post-1989, the constant silencing of her as a child and as a young woman, and the growing objectification of women's bodies. This is how *Rewolucja Balonowa* showed the multi-layered subordination of women's bodies as one of the consequences of 'freedom.'

Feminist interrogations of the relationship between transformation and approaches to sexuality in Polish society were also offered in two 2022 works by Agnieszka Jakimiak and Mateusz Atman, and by Agnieszka Wolny-Hamkało and Martyna Majewska. These artists presented the 1989 events as a lost opportunity to rethink sexuality, sex, gender, and, above all, human-to-human relations. On the other hand, however, gender and sexuality were proposed as critical frameworks to analyse transformation. Jakimiak and Atman – inspired by Stusińska's research (2021) – prepared *Miła Robótka*

(*A Nice Little Job*) for the Aleksander Fredro Theatre in Gniezno.[11] The piece explored how various narrations about and representations of sex, gender, and sexuality in post-1989 Poland – including some references to the 1993 ban on abortion – impacted approaches to sexuality in today's Polish society.

At the Jerzy Szaniawski Theatre in Wałbrzych, Wolny-Hamkało and Majewska staged *Niewolnica Isaura* (*The Slave Isaura*, 2022).[12] The production re-staged selected episodes of *Escrava Isaura* (*Isaura: Slave Girl*), the 1976 Brazilian telenovela first shown in Poland in 1985, episodes of which attracted, on average, 84 per cent of the Polish television audience (Maciejewski, 2005). Wolny-Hamkało and Majewska departed from asking why the series became iconic in 1980s and 1990s Poland. Their *Niewolnica Isaura* used cross-gender casting (Ireneusz Mosio played Izaura), songs, and metatheatrical references to reveal how the romanticisation of the unequal slave-master binary determined relations between women and men, and how the objectification of women underpinned Poles' mass-fascination with *Escrava Isaura*,; both are still evident in gender and sexual relations in contemporary Poland.

From a feminist perspective, what is significant about the productions narrating the 1989 transformation is that abortion – and the 1993 law – was never the primary topic. As observed by Ewelina Wejber-Wąsiewicz, unwanted pregnancy, for a very long time, was a marginal topic in contemporary Polish theatre (2015, p. 86). It was only after the 2016 debate about the further outlawing of abortion and its 2020 ban that theatre artists started exploring women's reproductive rights. However, as the Element's final section will show, the full potential of feminist engagement with abortion laws and the influence of the Catholic Church emerges in and through the transnational alliances of Ukrainian and Polish women.

Nevertheless, I want to highlight one production in which the 1993 anti-abortion law was included as part of (hi)stories of women in Poland seen as permanent and repeated acts of women being betrayed by politicians (Graff, 2024, p. 9). *Have a good cry* by Magda Szpecht, Weronika Pelczyńska and Lena Schimscheiner at the Scena Robocza in Poznań used elements of clowning and stand-up to interrogate the discourses related to abortion in Poland's history post-1993. The production referenced – through video material – the 1992 moment when the new anti-abortion law was announced. However, the focus was the personal, social, and political costs of the 1993 and 2020 anti-abortion laws, as seen by young women directly affected by the bans. Their production connected to the narratives of the subordination of women's bodies as the

---

[11] For the trailer see: www.youtube.com/watch?v=5xDgNOLK474.
[12] For the trailer see: www.youtube.com/watch?v=fJE_mRXgmNQ.

consequence of the 1989 transformation. However, Szpecht, Pelczyńska, and Schimscheiner also announced their right to reclaim their political and personal agency over their bodies.[13]

2.3 *1989*: Herstories of Polish Women's Transgenerational Fights for Freedoms

To consolidate my reflections on how women theatre makers engaged with sexuality, gender, and age to perform diverse and multivocal Herstories of Poland's transformation, in this part I explore how the different tropes and tendencies discussed thus far are brought together and developed through the transmedia project *1989*.

1989 was a collaboratively written musical that premiered at the end of 2022. It mixed rap with popular music from Poland's 1980s and 1990s.[14] The authors were director Katarzyna Szyngiera, cultural studies scholar Marcin Napiórkowski, journalist and reporter Mirosław Wlekły, and Hip-Hop musician Andrzej 'Webber' Mikosz.[15] In addition, individual Polish rap artists wrote selected songs. The choreographer was Barbara Olech and the scenographer was Milena Czarnik. Two theatres collaborated as producers – the Juliusz Słowacki Theatre from Kraków and the Gdański Shakespeare Theatre. Later, the authors published a book (Napiórkowski, Szyngiera and Wlekły, 2024), to scope out the context of the musical and to reflect on the process of collecting historical material. The Słowacki and Shakespeare theatres produced official music videos of selected songs, and an album of the musical's songs was released on CD and online.[16] An audience of 824,000 people watched the live televised version on TVP1, the free-to-air main channel of Polish national television.[17]

I am emphasising how *1989* was dispersed across multiple authors and media because it spoke to and reinforced the core concerns of the project: (1) constructing a historical narrative through multivoicedness enabled by perspectives of different women, (2) allowing these perspectives to rethink collective

---

[13] For more, see 'Theatre As a Platform for Women's Anger, Co-Participation and the Creating of Alternative Realities: Interview with Magda Szpecht' at www.cambridge.org/Ewa.

[14] For the trailer see: www.youtube.com/watch?v=oovmW6JOPQM and www.youtube.com/watch?v=7UG4aQwxq5I.

[15] Hip Hop and rap are global cultural movements that grew out of Black American culture and has been appropriated by White artists. However, as shown by Milosz Miszczynski and Adriana Helbig, Europe's Hip Hop has (generally) moved on from an appropriation of African American culture and developed localised styles and aesthetics (2017, p. 7).

[16] For the music videos see for example: www.youtube.com/watch?reload=9&v=16gg47PpvuU; for the music album see: https://open.spotify.com/album/2LeO9OHltJXAdXOzdyU4Pv.

[17] The live broadcast happened on 27th of May 2024 at 8 pm. To put the numbers into context, at a similar time, 1,346,202 people watched the main evening news programme on the main Polish public channel (TVP1). These numbers come from the reports by Poland's National Broadcasting Agency.

memories related to the events, (3) inviting different audiences to participate in this reinterpretation, and, through all of this, (4) rethinking the homosocial community envisioned by the Romantic paradigm, displaced by one whose strength resides in multiplicity and difference, and its women.[18]

The plot centres on the story of Poland in the 1980s and Solidarność; the dramatic action finishes with the 4th of June 1989 election, which was the symbolic end of communism in Poland. The stories *1989* tells are told from the perspectives of wives and daughters – the wives of its most well-known leaders, particularly Gaja Kuroń (Magdalena Osińska), Krystyna Frasyniuk (Katarzyna Zawiślak-Dolny), and Danuta Wałęsa (Karolina Kazoń), and the daughters of Krystyna and Władysław Frasyniuk (Julia Latosińska).

The premise of the production – one that immediately announced its dialogue with the Romantic paradigm and its martyrology – was the hugely advertised aim to construct a positive 'myth' about Polish history that could bring people together. This sounds naïve, but for the authors – as Szyngiera reflected during the European Theatre Forum (2023) and which was also evident in the production – the positive myth was not simply about the victory against communism and thus redefining the Romantic paradigm of a fight that always ends with a male death. The penultimate song, 'Co jeśli się uda' ('What if we succeed') – written by Polish rapper Łona – delivered a 'prophetic' image of Poland after the transformation and the failed opportunity for a better and more equal society, one that respects differences. The song also spoke to the strong polarisation of Poland's society in the 2020s – grown out of the social rifts discussed in the introduction – which politicians used for political gain (Górska, 2019; Ruszkowski, Przestalski and Maranowski, 2020). This, in turn, made the production's definition of a positive myth even more potent: victory was enabled by people with *different ideas* about freedom finding a way to work together. These included the socialist ideas of Jacek Kuroń (Marcin Czarnik), the capitalist dreams of Władysław Frasyniuk (Mateusz Bieryt), his daughter's (Julia Latosińska) wish to play with her dad, the new generation's visions of Poland with birthdays in McDonald's, and the dreams of a family in which partners shared daily chores and raised children together sung about by Kazoń as Danuta Wałęsa and Zawiślak-Dolny as Krystyna Frasyniuk.

The interweaving of ideas, stories, and contexts in *1989* worked in different ways and on multiple levels, the realisation of which heavily depended on the collaborative authorship of the production (see Figure 1). A case in point is the scene in which women and men debated the future of Poland. The scene was set in the apartment of Gaja and Jacek Kuroń. The female and male leaders of

---

[18] I have analysed some (different) aspects of the musical and its focus on women's voices in the review written for *Didaskalia* (Lech, 2024a).

Figure 1 Scenography by Milena Czarnik enables '1989' its multivocal engagement with the transformation. Photo by Bartek Barczyk for the Juliusz Słowacki Theatre in Kraków.

Solidarność occupied the living room, while Gaja, Krystyna, and Danuta were in the kitchen. The scenographer Milena Czarnik ensured that the audience tuned into and gazed on the women in the kitchen, placing them centre stage while the living room was upstage to the right. The spectators did not hear the majority of what was being said in the living room; this was narrated by the song performed by Kazoń, Zawiślak-Dolny, and Osińska, in which they sang about what the future would look like for them. This song's refrain underscored the idea that all visions for the future were to be considered equal as well as reinforcing the need for the community to come together:

> You sketch the future on a napkin
> And you dream of it finally coming true.
> Everyone's heart tells them what to change
> But we need more of us to make those dreams come true.
>   (Napiórkowski, Szyngiera and Wlekły, 2023, p. 89)

A further example of intertwining stories and experiences is that of the Frasyniuk Family and their songs that repeated each other's melodic lines, although in different keys. Bieryt, as Władysław, sang about his dream of life in the 'West' (beyond the Iron Curtain). Zawiślak-Dolny, as Krystyna, sang about the loneliness of not knowing if her fugitive husband was alive.

Latosińska, as their daughter, sang about learning to read as a child by reading her mother's suicide notes. Music by Andrzej 'Webber' Mikosz brought these texts together, and placed an emphasis on the young girl's fight for survival and how it was underpinned by her father's dreams and her mother's fears. Latosińska sang:

> She swallows the prescribed medication with a bottle of wine,
> Again, the ambulance's sound, again, 'she is alive'.
> I've forgiven you for being gone, Daddy,
> You're fighting for tomorrow, and I must survive today.
> I know it's all for us
> That the future is destined to be wonderful,
> I can't be thankful for this . . . .
> I'm a child; I want to play with my Dad . . .
> (Napiórkowski, Szyngiera and Wlekły, 2023, pp. 107–108)

This further exemplifies how *1989* foregrounded the different efforts, losses, and sacrifices women made to fight for freedom – a fight that was not necessarily on the front line but was always about surviving and enabling others to survive. In *1989*, women were shown fighting for freedom by raising children, finding food to feed families, ringing an ambulance to save dying mothers, striking, saving men, protesting, and hiding clandestine leaflets between sanitary pads that communist policemen were reluctant to check. At the same time, the production highlighted moments in which women's leadership ensured that Solidarność survived. For example, as the actors sang about the start of the strikes in the shipyard in August 1980, the change in rhythm from long to short lines emphasised that it was Henryka Krzywonos who stopped the tram. As Dominika Feiglewicz as Krzywonos appeared, the actors sang: 'This is Henryka Krzywonos/ the woman tram driver comes to the rescue' (Napiórkowski, Szyngiera and Wlekły, 2023, p. 81).

Linking women's different agencies and survival-focused efforts additionally strengthened the production's rejection of Polish martyrology and its celebration of men who died in the name of national freedom. This rejection was also evident in the show's explicit engagement with and critique of the Romantic paradigm, for example, when the chorus of women recalled multiple symbols of Polish heroic male fights and deaths, expressing the hope that Poland could become a country that did not only remember its past sufferings but also looked to a more hopeful future. At the same time, the production eschewed romanticisation of the female figures by highlighting their struggles and humanity. The latter, for example, was evinced by the inclusion of their sexual relations in the history of transformation. For instance, one of the first scenes between Danuta and Lech Wałęsa ended with Danuta's orgasm performed by Kazoń, which challenged the asexual image of the 'Polish Mother'.

The agencies of diverse women, their different heroisms, and their interrelations with each other, and with different stories and silences, came particularly to the fore in two songs: when Danuta Wałęsa delivered the Nobel award speech and, later, when women prisoners sang about fighting for freedom. The Nobel song built on a fragment from Danuta Wałęsa's autobiography in which she confessed: 'Performing on the Nobel podium, I did not feel like Wałęsa's wife or a housewife. I felt like a Polish woman representing other Polish women' (Wałęsa, 2011, p. 157). In *1989*, Kazoń as Wałęsa sang the Noble Speech that Danuta Wałęsa could have delivered on 10 December 1983 if she had been allowed to speak on her behalf. The song was written, as the authors stated, for all women in Solidarność (Napiórkowski, Szyngiera and Wlekły, 2024, p. 305).

In the speech, Kazoń-Wałęsa sang about women's rights not being considered human rights.[19] She linked this to the invisible everyday heroism and intersectional marginalisations that Polish women faced as mothers, wives, women, and 'Eastern Europeans.' This connection was emphasised towards the end of the song as the entire female cast joined Kazoń, and together they announced: 'It's Us!' which Karolina Kamińska as Alina Pienkowska completes: 'The half of Solidarność' (Napiórkowski, Szyngiera and Wlekły, 2023, p. 118). As they sang, Napiórkowski's text and Barbara Olech's choreography (through gestures) referenced the 2016 and 2020 women's protests against the abortion ban. In the musical's album, the choreographic gestures were replaced by references to the 2020 protests – specifically the line: Wypierdalać (Get the fuck out of here), directed at politicians who refused women the freedom of choice. A link to the abortion ban was also made in a line sung by Dominika Feiglewicz (Krzywonos) voicing a description of Solidarność's women: 'The half that does not claim / the right to make someone else's life' (Napiórkowski, Szyngiera and Wlekły, 2023, p. 118). At this stage of the performance, the spectators had already learned about Krzywonos losing her baby because she was beaten up by communist police for leading strikes. Thus, the line carried the connotation of men granting themselves the right to decide whether a woman could or could not give birth.

Hence, when Kazoń-Wałęsa sang the final lines of the Noble speech, the statement she made had transtemporal relevance; it also spoke to how it was not only women who were silenced in Poland's recent history:

> I collect this award representing all women
> All children, all excluded.

---

[19] The scene – adapted into a music video and featuring Danuta Wałęsa herself – is available to view online: www.youtube.com/watch?v=7pR72KElU5U.

> Not as someone's wife but as a human
> We do not have to hide because we are invisible
> The world will never know us.
> So, I raise our cause, I proclaim our praise,
> In this never-delivered speech
> So that in the future, it will be remembered that not only men
> Fought to change the world
> So that not only men about men
> Tell the story for generations to come.

Giving voice to the Solidarność women and women's protests against abortions made resonant a transgenerational history of Polish women – different generations at different times, fighting against patriarchal and nationalistic acts of violence. More specifically, *1989* made references to medieval witch hunts, Nazism, Stalinism, and fighting for reproductive rights, children's rights, and the environment. One missed opportunity was the lack of reference to the patriarchal violence and oppression committed by the Catholic Church against women.

The show's transgenerational dimension related to the way in which the production aimed to be accessible to generationally different audience constituencies, from those with memories of Solidarność to those born after 1989. This was evident in archaisms such as the 'translation' of certain historical characters into contemporary celebrities popular amongst teenagers, which helped to situate them within the story – references that were not necessarily grasped by older generations. In other words, it was difficult to fully understand the production without talking to people of different ages. After the first performance I viewed with my cousins (aged nineteen and fourteen) in Wrocław in March 2023, they proudly explained some contemporary references to their confused parents but, at the same time, had many questions about the historical figures such as Wojciech Jaruzelski. The point is that *1989* was not only written collaboratively, but also created to generate intergenerational conversation about Poland, in which everyone 'owned' some but not the whole (hi)story. The transmedia aspect of the project – the televised production, the book and the music album – strengthened this strategy.

Revealing how Poland's transformation had the potential to but ultimately failed to facilitate a new political imagination – a very different one from that proposed by *Dziady* – the production ended with a song, which reminded the audience they once again had the opportunity to change history:

> The wind of history is once again blowing,
> It carries us into the future
> I have hope, the time has come
> It's happening; enough darkness already.
> (Napiórkowski, Szyngiera and Wlekły, 2023, p. 133)

The immediate context was the 2023 election – in which the far-right was defeated largely due to the women's vote – but the need for a new community and the audience's co-responsibility in shaping it goes beyond the election.

Hence, the political and cultural value of the different 'feminist imaginings' of Poland's community created through Herstories and interrogations of collective memory related to the 1989 transformation, as discussed in this Section. Polish women's defiance of invisibility, oppression, and objectification grounded in national history and struggles for independence as fuel for feminist imaginings forms the bridge to Section 3 with its focus on Ukrainian artists.

3 Women in War Taking the Agency Back

Ewa Bal

As headlined in the introduction, the most important sociocultural changes in Ukraine during the transition period did not begin immediately after the country regained its independence in 1991, but only after 2014. They were linked to the social mobilisation that accompanied the Ukrainian Revolution of Dignity and the shock of Russia's retaliation: the annexation of Crimea and the separation of parts of the Donetsk and Luhansk regions from the rest of Ukraine, which was the de facto beginning of the war that continues to this day. These dramatic events, accumulated over time, became an impulse for Ukrainian artists to engage in the so-called 'coming out of silence' (Matusiak, 2020, Harbuzyuk, 2023a), that is, working through the traumas of the twentieth century, which had a far-reaching impact on the state of Ukraine, but which could not previously be debunked due to the still effective mechanisms of post-colonial dependence on Russia. These include events such as the Holodomor (the great famine of 1932–1933 caused by Stalin's restrictive policies towards the Ukrainian peasantry in the east of the country), the Second World War, or the Chernobyl nuclear power plant disaster (caused by failures on the part of the Soviet authorities that were carefully concealed from Ukrainians and the world).

According to Matusiak and Harbuzyuk, coming to terms with this repression was a prerequisite for post-traumatic psychosocial growth, equivalent to the process of decolonisation. However, while this post-traumatic growth is well suited to describing the motivations of older generations of creators, now in their fifties and sixties, whose biographies were partly intertwined with the times of the USSR, it is inappropriate for the generational changing of the guard that took place in Ukraine in 2014, associated with the rise of the 'self-made' generation (Bal, 2024b). These latter artists (now in their thirties and forties), already born in independent Ukraine, gained experience based on educational models other than the Soviet one, took part in internships and residencies abroad, from which they drew impulses to fight for gender equality issues and LGBTQ+ rights. Their political consciousness was formed during the 2013–2014 Revolution of Dignity, a revolt against the pro-Russian policies of Viktor Yanukovych and the inefficiency of the Ukrainian state, which was riddled with corruption, nepotism, and patriarchal power relations.[20] Young people experienced the violence of this system first-hand – initially on Independence Maidan, where 100 people were killed by the bullets of pro-regime gendarmes. And later during the Donbas war, where one of the main tools of the Russian-backed struggle was rape and torture, inflicted on both men and women. This knowledge, however, rarely spread beyond the borders of Ukraine. And it was only after 24 February 2022, when reports from Bucha, Irpin, Hostomel,[21] and Mariupol[22] came out, the whole world saw that rape culture and violence, including against children, have become a notorious feature of Russia's war tactics.

Therefore, it is important to emphasise that already after 2014, dissent against rape and humiliation became the main driving force behind the actions of the 'self-made' generation, whose exponents were primarily women. Their breaking of the silence led to a feminist turn in Ukrainian theatre aimed at the very foundations of post-Soviet patriarchy. To explain this turn, it is more advantageous to draw on Judith Butler's theorisation of the performativity of discourses and bodies than the psychoanalytic tools of trauma research. Butler's work enables us to understand why violence inflicted in words, discourses and also directly, as a physical violation of the body, can lead, on the one hand, to the subordination and precariousness of subjects and, on the other, to a response and reaction that undermines the authority of power.

Speaking of hate speech, Butler emphasised: 'The utterances of hate speech are part of the continuous and uninterrupted process to which we are subjected, an on-going subjection (assujetissement) that is the very operation of interpellation, that continuously repeated action of discourse by which subjects are formed in subjugation' (Butler, 1997, p. 27). At the same time, however, 'the injurious address may appear to fix or paralyse the one it

---

[20] For more information see the documentary: *Winter on Fire: Ukraine's Fight for Freedom* (2015) directed by Evgeny Afineevsky, produced by Netflix et al., Ukraine, United States, United Kingdom, distributed by Netflix.

[21] For more information about Bucha massacre, and Hostomel battle see: www.bbc.com/news/world-europe-61667500.

[22] For more information see the movie: *20 Days in Mariupol* (2023) directed by Mstyslav Chernov, produced by Associated Press, PBS Frontline, distributed by PBS Distribution, Link to the trailer: https://www.youtube.com/watch?v=9H_Fg_5x4ME.

hails, but it may also produce an unexpected and enabling response. If to be addressed is to be interpellated, then the offensive call runs the risk of inaugurating a subject in speech who comes to use language to counter the offensive call' (p. 2). The political possibility of reworking the force of the speech act against the force of injury consists of misappropriating the force of speech from those prior contexts (p. 40). In other words, Butler suggests that the same force that validates the action of oppressive discourses can, with appropriate subversive reworking, serve to negate their onto-epistemic underpinnings. Thus, by transferring the mechanism described by Butler to the field of reflection on the agency of the performing arts, I will show how, in the specific case of Ukraine, theatre transforms the effects of hate speech and rape culture into strategy of resistance.

In many of her reflections, Butler points to the regularity with which the performativity of discourses is usually reinforced by the performativity of bodies (Butler, 1997, 2011, 2015). Indeed, she draws attention to the various ways in which precarious bodies appear in public space, whether in the form of physical gatherings, photographic or media representations. More generally, the body, its gender and sexuality are sometimes defined by both discourse and action. Bodily acts, like linguistic acts, retain in their representations the possibility of intervening in the system that defines them. They have the power to dismantle patriarchy because the field of recognition imposed on bodies (and thus the normativity of body, gender, sexuality, race, and class produced in the process of iterative performance) and the right to appear can be skilfully overridden or unsealed by the marginalised subjects themselves (Butler, 2015, p. 47). The performativity of the body 'produces a rupture within the sphere of appearance, exposing the contradiction by which its claim to universality is posited and nullified. There can be no entry into the sphere of appearance without a critique of the differential forms of power by which that sphere is constituted' (p. 50).

With the notion of 'cracking the field of recognition' (Bal, 2023a) or 'a rift within the sphere of appearance' (Butler, 2015, p. 50), it is, therefore, better to explain the process of women's coming to the fore in Ukraine as they exposed the deeply rooted rape culture in post-Soviet society – as a war tactic to subjugate another. In this section, I examine the main stages of this 'breaking out of the silence' in Ukrainian theatre by women, starting with dramas and plays produced in the early stages of the Russian-Ukrainian war, such as Natalia Vorozhbyt's play *Pohani Dorohy* (*Bad Roads,* 2017) and the production *H-effect* (2020), which undermine the patriarchal foundations of nationalism. Thereafter, I turn to productions created after the full-scale Russian invasion of Ukraine, performances which express thunderous chants in response to the violence of the Russian military against Ukrainian women and children: *Vertep* (*Nativity Scene*, 2022), directed by Oksana Dmitriieva, and *Matki. Pieśń na Czas Wojny* (*Mothers. Song for a Wartime*, 2023), directed by Marta Górnicka.

3.1 Without Love and without Heroes

One of the first theatrical testimonies to the war in Donbass is Natalia Vorozhbyt's play *Bad Roads* (2017),[23] also brought to the screen in 2020 by the author.[24] Here, I refer to the Ukrainian production of the play, directed by Tamara Trunova in 2019 for the Theatre on the Left Bank of the Dnieper in Kyiv.[25] In this production, the director succeeded in bringing out a specific aspect of the impact of war: the dismantling of culturally established ideas about love, femininity, masculinity, and heroism, regardless of which side of the armed conflict.

The play opens with a scene dominated by one element of the set: a metal fence running across the stage. The actors moving in front of and behind it rarely manage to reach the other side. The only way to connect the two areas is through a locked gate and a slippery slide: you can climb over it, only to slide down again a moment later. For the local audience, this was a clear reference to the Donbas region, which is sometimes perceived as governed by its own rules, an island cut off from the rest of Ukraine (in Ukrainian it is said 'na Donbasi', and the preposition 'na' is usually combined with islands). On a more general level, however, the wall is simply an obstacle: to communication and human relations.

The axis of the plot is the journey of 40-year-old Natasha, a Kyiv journalist who wants to write a report on the war going on in Donbas since 2014. Her perspective of disillusionment with everything she has known so far about the ethos of the army, love, and sex between a man and a woman, projects the tone of the next six scenes of theatrical reportage. In the opening monologue, the tall and statuesque Natasha (played by Oksana Cherkashyna), dressed in an elegant red coat and high-heeled shoes, surrounded by a chorus of young girls and men, recounts her meeting with a Ukrainian officer who is to be her guide in the Donbas. She speaks of the man as if he were the object of her love, although the source of her imagery is popular Ukrainian and Russian patriotic songs from

---

[23] The play was written in 2017, commissioned by the Royal Court Theatre in London, and premiered there. Following its UK premiere, it has also been staged in Ukraine and Poland (Bal, 2023a, p. 89).

[24] *Bad Roads*, 2020, written and directed by Natalia Vorozhbyt, produced by Kristi Films, Ukraine, distributed by Netflix.

[25] For the trailer see: www.dramox.tv/preview/332-bad-roads.

the Soviet era. The choir that surrounds Natasha interrupts her monologue from time to time, singing songs about women's supposed weakness for men in uniform, ironically counterpointing her point of view. Natasha herself realises that her imaginings have little to do with reality, as her companion, focused on military tasks and reflexive daily activities, has obvious problems communicating his own needs, expressing tenderness and achieving sexual arousal. When the two finally find themselves alone in a hotel room, the only form of sexual excitement he can muster, to the woman's astonishment, is to force Natasha into a humiliating position on her knees and perform fellatio, for which he rewards her with a necklace of a trident (a symbol of Ukrainian independence).

This shocking final of the affair overturns common perceptions of both the heroism and nobility of soldiers and of devoted women yearning for love. And it is mirrored in Tamara Trunova's play in the relationship between the young women of Donbas and the soldiers fighting on the side of the Russian-backed separatists of the Donetsk People's Republic. In one of the final scenes, three young girls in airy white summer dresses are competing to see who will get the better gift from their military lover. After some discussion, it becomes clear that giving their bodies to soldiers is indeed painful and humiliating. However, they are unable to treat their own bodies subjectively because they have not been taught or been accustomed to tenderness in the family. In this way, Natalia Vorozhbyt shows how far family and social ties have been eroded by death, illness, and poverty, and how young people are not given the attention they deserve. In one scene we see a young girl, waiting for a soldier to arrive, talking to her mentally absent, TV-obsessed grandmother, who only ostensibly looks after her granddaughter after the death of her parents. Trunova and Vorozhbyt make it clear to the audience that the answer to this breakdown of social bonds is, unfortunately, sexual violence against women, which they themselves mistakenly recognise as a normative manifestation of physical closeness.

This seemingly hopeless situation, however, paves the way for a specific subversion, that is, a repetition of the scenario of carnal humiliation and violation by women, which could have the effect of undermining the very foundations of rape culture. To explain and elaborate: in one scene, a young girl kidnapped by separatists has to give herself to a soldier in order to 'buy' her way out of captivity with her body. Left alone with him, she begins to play the role of a submissive woman used to humiliation and violence, convincing the man that she is doing all this out of love for him. Surprised by this behaviour, the man is unable to achieve sexual arousal, as he is apparently only accustomed to acts of violence in his relationships with women. In performance, the man on stage loses control of the situation for a moment and, in his only 'human reflex', helps the girl to wash herself in the bathtub (even though it was his aggression that made the girl pee herself out of fear). He also joins her in the bath, as if the shared bath of executioner and victim were a guarantee of his moral catharsis. In the film version of her play, Natalia Vorozhbyt gives this scene another dimension; instead of forgiving the man, she restores the girl's agency: The man falls asleep for a moment in the bathtub, and she, seizing the opportunity, smashes his head with a stone and runs away.

Thus, it is clear that the subversive performance of submission by the woman exposes, as Butler would say, the patriarchal power that inflicts suffering. This guerrilla tactic of acting as a weak, precarious subject in the field of the aggressor is at the same time the only effective form of defence where, in a direct confrontation, women have no chance of prevailing. It is worth adding that analogous guerrilla tactics, this time at the intersection of performance art, cyber-activism and investigative journalism, have recently been used, for example, by performers from the Vaba Lava Narva Theatre and the Polish-Estonian artistic collective in the production *Spy Girls* (2024), directed by Magda Szpecht, a Pole, according to a script by Olga Drygas.[26] In order to create the dramaturgy of the play, the performers opened fake female accounts on the Russian portal Vkontakte for a period of three months and, in the 'Dating' tab, paired up with Russian soldiers who eagerly sent them their photos and told them where they were based. Using this tactic, the performers found out not only where Russian troops were stationed, but also where their ammunition depots were. They then passed this information on to the Ukrainian army. Guerrilla tactics, acting in the field of the aggressor, performative repetition, thus open up the possibility of initiating effective resistance.[27]

3.2 Reworking through Scenarios of Failure and Victimhood

But guerrilla resistance is not always enough or effective. Sometimes the war forces young people to admit defeat or to face their own weaknesses. This aspect of negative performativity – showing the intention of actions and their unfortunate nature – was the inspiration for the production *H-effect* (2021), directed by the Ukrainian artist Roza Sarkisian and the Polish playwright, the late Joanna Wichowska (in private life Roza's partner).[28] Both used Heiner Müller's reading of Hamlet as a starting point for their devised dramaturgy, which explores how young Ukrainians situate themselves in relation to the iconic figure of male failure, that is, Hamlet, and the iconic figure of female subordination – Ophelia.[29] Director and dramaturg wanted their actors to think

---

[26] For the trailer see: youtu.be/QWsQ9zhD6k4?si=qubdodr5fBo6vUYi.
[27] For more, see 'Theatre As a Platform for Women's Anger, Co-Participation and the Creating of Alternative Realities: Interview with Magda Szpecht' at www.cambridge.org/Ewa.
[28] For the trailer see: www.youtube.com/watch?v=ueNIqemBc2Y.
[29] My analysis of this production comes from the recently published article: Bal, 2024b, *Ukrainian Gambit. Postcolonial Perspectives on The First Shakespeare Theatre Festival in Ukraine,*

about who Hamlet is today, in 2020, and for whose fathers Hamlet should fight in the light of the Donbas war that has been going on since 2014. In other words, how they situate themselves in relation to the challenges of patriotism.

To this end Sarkisian and Wichowska invited several mostly professional actors from different regions of Ukraine, different backgrounds and sexual orientations, speaking different languages: Russian and Ukrainian. By gathering them on stage under their first and last names, they wanted to retrieve the actors' autoethnographic perspective on the war.[30] There is Yaroslav (Slavik) Havyanets, a 20-year-old man from western Ukraine, a defender of Donetsk airport who was captured and tortured by separatists; there is Roman Kryvdyk, a professional actor and combat medic who is appalled by the atrocities on the front line; there is Kateryna Kotlyarova, a volunteer soldier who talks out about sexism in the army, and Oleg-Rodion Shuryhin-Herkalov, a Donetsk native, Russian-speaking and openly gay who sews uniforms for the army, and finally, as previously mentioned, Oksana Cherkashyna, a prominent actress from Kharkiv who refuses to accept the war situation in Ukraine, where women are rape victims, and decides to leave for Poland.

They all have very individual and very different views on the ongoing war – but they all share PTSD syndromes.[31] On stage, they search for a way to express what they feel through their bodies and words, starting with the phrase 'I am Hamlet, because . . . . '. This sentence is at the same time an admission of failure, of weakness, a sentence that gives them the right to speak the truth. After all, not everyone is like Slavik, one of the so-called 'cyborgs', that is, those brave soldiers who refused to surrender in 2014 while defending the Donetsk airport from the separatist attack. Cyborgs failed only because a bombed-out tower collapsed on their heads. But even Slavik reveals his vulnerability when, in the presence of the audience, he relives a scene, deliberately recorded by the separatists and posted on a YouTube channel, in which he is ordered to kill a comrade-in-arms. He doesn't obey the order, but the risk of losing his own life was extremely high.

Katya, for her part, joined the Ukrainian army as a volunteer, but had to admit that women in the trenches must be aware of the extremely patriarchal treatment

---

Critical Stages/Scènes critiques, 30 December 2024, www.critical-stages.org/30/ukrainian-gambit-decolonial-perspectives-on-the-first-shakespeare-theatre-festival-in-ukraine/.

[30] Thanks to the fact that the process of working on the stage was accompanied by a film camera (Elwira Niewiera and Piotr Rosolowski shot 'a making of' documentary *The Hamlet Syndrome*, 2022), we learn who specifically takes part in the performance.

[31] Post-traumatic stress disorder – a psychiatric disorder that is a form of reaction to an extremely stressful event (trauma) that exceeds a person's ability to cope and adapt. See: *Klasyfikacja zaburzeń psychicznych i zaburzeń zachowania w ICD-10*, Kraków-Warszawa: Uniwersyteckie Wydawnictwo Medyczne "Vesalius", 1998, p. 96–97.

and constantly prove their combat usefulness. However, in her improvised performance, she demonstrates out loud her profound patriotism and dedication to the Ukrainian flag, a sacred totem for those on the front lines. This is why she cannot understand Oksana Cherkashyna, for whom the same flag, representing patriotism, becomes a gag in her mouth during a rape scene. On stage, Cherkashyna holds this flag in her mouth, wraps it around her head or ties her hands with it, pantomiming the passive response of the female body to an act of collective violence. By this, she is asking, whether being a rape victim could be considered the same patriotic act as fighting on the front line? Or is this rape only an inadmissible act of humiliation and violence? Unable to find answers to these questions, and at the same time uncomfortable with the possibility of being a victim, she decides to leave the country. What becomes clear to the spectator is that women's war testimonies on stage are challenging the limits of patriotism, which is associated with patriarchal power.

Crucial to understanding this production, however, is the attitude of Oleg-Rodion Shuryhin-Herkalov, who at one point appears on stage in a white wedding dress, 'disguised' for the audience as Ophelia. In his monologue, he convincingly explains that despite his sexual orientation and his struggle since childhood with signs of homophobia (including acts of physical aggression) from those closest to him, he does not want to be treated as a victim, nor does he crave the paternalistic compassionate gaze of those who would see his fate as a precariously exposed body. On the contrary, he insists that the ongoing war reinforces in him a sense of subjectivity and strength, as he states: 'the aggressor's violence cannot inflict on me more cruelty than I have already experienced or suffered in my life'. Oleg thus rips off from himself the Ophelia's white wedding dress, in order to overcome the fear of a much stronger external opponent.

Thus, by means of this act or action, Oleg redefines the ontological foundations of the precarious body. Because, as Butler would put it: The 'frames' that work to differentiate the lives we can apprehend from those we cannot (or that produce lives across a continuum of life) not only organize visual experience but also generate specific ontologies of the subject (Butler 2010, p. 3). Beings not worthy of the name of life, precarious subjects in this framework are not grievable. These normative conditions for the production of the subject allow historically contingent ontology, such that our very capacity to discern and name the 'being' of the subject is dependent on norms that facilitate that recognition. Oleg takes on the agency of active resistance to those norms that constitute his/her victimhood, and actually proposes a different ontology of the subject: as a fashion stylist, he decides to sew uniforms for the Ukrainian army. In doing so, he undermines the ontoepistemic basis of passive resistance, as exemplified by the female characters in Natalia Vorozhbyt's *Bad Roads*. Under the conditions of war, Ophelia's agency, driven by the ontoepistemic condition of victimhood, is substituted by a forceful response, in active fight.

In fact, many Ukrainian female artists and representatives of the LBTGQ+ community, joined the army after the full-scale Russian attack on Ukraine on the 24th of February 2022. They gave first-hand accounts from the front lines of the ongoing war, but also disarmed patriarchal stereotypes about the non-heteronormative and female presence in the army, and redefined the role of performative arts during the war. In one of the plays directed by Roza Sarkisian in 2023, with the perverse title *Fucking Truffaut* (2023) – which queerly joins the debate on strategies of the overrepresentation of war – Antonina Romanov (a queer performer currently fighting in the army) makes a kind of self-declaration, recorded on video, on behalf of the theatre makers.[32] In it, she stresses that she herself made many anti-war performances during the early stages of the war against Russia. Today, however, when the war machine is in full swing, pacifism in the theatre can be harmful, because it works mainly in favour of the aggressor in the minds of the audience (Bal, 2024a). Most theatre productions, including those by women, therefore, while taking a stand on the ongoing war, no longer question the need to defend the homeland. If the word 'patria' is understood literally as the homeland – the land of the fathers – then the call to defend it is the call of patriarchy. But Russia's full-scale attack on Ukraine has certainly changed the attitude of Ukrainian society towards the national community and the country in a positive way: to respond to this challenge with readiness to fight.

However, in the meantime, another aspect of war came to light: the relation between rape culture and the fate of mothers and children from areas afflicted by war and now occupied by the Russians.

3.3 Mothers Strike Back

Almost from the first day of Russia's full-scale attack on Ukraine, there was a wave of women and children fleeing the war in Europe, as men of age were banned from leaving the country due to the need to defend it. The image of the bombed-out theatre in Mariupol, where civilians had taken refuge in the basement, having previously made a bird's-eye sign on the floor with the word 'children' written on it, has become a symbol of the war. They hoped, unfortunately in vain, for humane behaviour on the part of the invaders, despite the fact that, according to an investigation by Amnesty International, the Russians had

---

[32] For the trailer see: www.youtube.com/watch?v=2h3ETkSyygA.

deliberately dropped several bombs on the building by detonating them simultaneously.³³ The Russians have also carried out and continue to carry out kidnappings of Ukrainian children, who are subjected to severe indoctrination, identity change processes, and illegal adoption on Russian territory.³⁴ It is estimated that the Russians have already abducted around 20,000 minors from Ukrainian territory, making it very difficult to reunite them with family members in Ukraine or to establish their whereabouts.³⁵ For these very crimes against children, the International Criminal Court (ICC) has issued arrest warrants for Vladimir Putin and Russia's Children's Ombudsman, Maria Lvova-Belova, declaring that their conduct constitutes genocide, committed with intent to destroy, in whole or in part, a nation or ethnic group. (Borger, 2022).

Art, cinema, and theatre also played a role in denouncing these crimes. On the one hand, they tried to provide a cognitive framework to this tragedy. On the other hand, theatre productions with Ukrainian women and children, created throughout Europe as a gesture of solidarity with Ukraine, appealed to the consciousness of Europeans for the necessary support of Ukraine. In order to illustrate these strategies, I refer to the performance *Vertep* (*Nativity scene*, 2023) directed by Oksana Dmitriieva from the Kharkiv Puppet Theatre, named after Afanasiev, and the performance *Mothers. A Song for a War Time* (2023) directed by Marta Górnicka (produced by the Chorus of Women Foundation, Teatr Powszechny in Warsaw, Maxim Gorki Theater in Berlin).³⁶

The theatre artists discussed thus far mostly used dramaturgies created on the basis of journalistic research and reports, or devised dramaturgies: based on auto-ethnographic improvisations of the actors. Oksana Dmitriieva, the Ukrainian theatre director, approaches the subject differently, usually using allegorical parables in theatre that can be read by both adult and young audiences and which avoid direct reference to traumatic experiences. Using plastic installations, animated puppets and props, Dmitriieva 'takes' the experience of violence against women and children out of the 'framework of war' (Butler, 2010a) and places it within the cognitive framework of parables that give it a symbolic, more universal meaning. Of course, she does not completely dispense with references to the local context. While the war was in full swing, the director prepared a nativity play, called 'Vertep' in Ukrainian, traditionally performed at Christmas. Focusing on the biblical

---

³³ www.amnesty.org.pl/ukraina-smiercionosny-atak-na-teatr-w-mariupolu-zbrodnia-wojenna-sledztwo/.
³⁴ https://pl.wikipedia.org/wiki/Uprowadzenia_dzieci_podczas_rosyjskiej_inwazji_na_Ukrain%C4%99.
³⁵ https://en.wikipedia.org/wiki/Child_abductions_in_the_Russo-Ukrainian_War
³⁶ For the trailer see: www.youtube.com/watch?v=hCQ3m27ue-E.

story of the slaughter of the innocents, Dmitriieva wanted to express on stage the grief of mothers at the loss of their children.

In the play, a mask animated by the actors, resembling a skull and embodying the power of evil, is responsible for the slaughter. And the world in which the saviour arrives is created on stage by means of wooden planks with handles, which, depending on the scene, become the buildings of Kharkiv in the hands of the actors, or tanks or cannons that 'shoot' human figures: as when the actors impale the figures on the stick of a tank 'barrel'. The central prop that draws the audience's attention to the performance is a large string of red beads worn by women in traditional Ukrainian folk costumes. It was strung across almost the entire width of the stage, as if encircling the neck of the entire country (Ukraine is grammatically feminine). Other strings of red beads are worn around the necks of the actresses playing the mothers of the murdered children. Mourning the loss of their children, they first let the red beads of the long necklace run down the string one by one, like drops of tears, and then scrub the boards of the stage with them, as if washing off the blood of their offspring. Finally, they roll the necklace into a ball and rock it like a child to sleep.

However, their pain is only alleviated when the evil is punished, and the corpse mask is cut off with a single slash of the angel saviour's sword. For a moment, the actor playing the angel holds up two sword-like planks which, together with his headdress, form the symbol of the trident – the emblem of Ukraine. Evil is thus opposed by Ukraine itself, which, for the audience, takes on the role of the biblical saviour – although, as the meaning of the necklace suggests, this saviour is a woman, a raped or wounded mother.

As can be seen, Dmitriieva dismantles rape culture differently from her predecessors, updating and reinterpreting mythologies and religious parables in her performances in a way that Rebecca Schneider has called 'reenactment' (Schneider, 2011). In contrast to the sometimes-naive art of reenacting battles by so-called reconstructionist, the reenactment she defines involves the reintroduction of elements of the archive into the realm of cultural practices. Drawing on Derrida's insights, Schneider elucidates how the archive has the forward-looking power to perform remnants. 'The elements of the archive that reappear in the repertoire of cultural practices carry the seeds of future scenarios and transformations' (Schneider, 2011, p. 108). Therefore, the performativity of the theatre lies in the evocation of the biblical story and its subsequent transformation as a future scenario. In the production I am discussing, this scenario is the promise of victory for Ukraine and the recovery of Ukrainian women's right to find their children or bury them with dignity.

Yet another possibility of resistance is offered by the Polish director Marta Górnicka in her recent production *Mothers. A Song for a Wartime* (2023), co-produced by the Teatr Powszechny in Warsaw and the Maxim Gorki Theater in Berlin, as well as the Chorus of Women Foundation. Like Dmitriieva, Górnicka is interested in the voices of women and children in wartime, but to express them she draws on the Maori danced song of New Zealand, 'haka', or the 'haka poi' performed by Maori women, characterised by warlike gestures, strong stomping and the fixing of a threatening gaze on the enemy. *Mother. A Song for a Wartime*, in 2023, toured theatres almost all over Europe, including the Avignon Theatre Festival. It starred women from Ukraine, Poland, and Belarus (where the political repression of Alexander Lukashenko's regime is still ongoing after the protests following the rigged presidential elections in 2020) who settled in Poland after the tragic events in their countries of origin, and whose accounts and personal experiences became part of the textual layer of the drama.

In the songs sung and danced by the women, Górnicka wanted to highlight the juxtaposition of two different ways of understanding the trauma of war. On the one hand, the actresses sing about the trauma of women and children who were raped or tortured in front of their loved ones during the war in Ukraine; a trauma that cannot be told in words, but only passed on in silence or carried in the body as a lifelong experience of death. On the other hand, the women repeat, in a somewhat ironic way, arguments about the trauma of the Second World War, which Western Europe has repressed over the last eighty years as a result of the economic boom of the Common Market. The consequence of this repression has been a rejection of thinking about the possibility of re-engagement in wartime conflict. 'This post-heroic mentality' – as Jürgen Habermas (2022) has aptly explained – 'was able to develop in Western Europe (...) during the second half of the twentieth century under the nuclear umbrella provided by the United States.' In *Mothers*, however, Górnicka contrasts this post-heroic attitude with the cries of aggrieved women calling on Western European societies to respond. And, as if hearing silence from the other side, they ironically hum Western Europe's children's lullaby to the well-known Polish tune 'Aaa, kotki dwa' (aaa, sleep my two little kittens), in which Górnicka has changed the words to 'Aaa, Europa'. The longer Europe remains in a state of lethargy, oblivious to the crumbling world it has created, the more it risks its very existence.

As can be seen from these examples, the performative power of representations of war from the point of view of precarious and fragile subjects extends along an axis that accommodates both guerrilla tactics, that is, the action of a weak subject in the enemy field (*Bad Roads, Spy Girls*), and the admission of defeat and doubt, or the rejection of such attitudes in favour of active combat

(*H-effect*, *Mothers. A Song for a Wartime*, *Vertep*). At the same time, the performances I have analysed make it necessary to include the perspective of those subjects who, unlike the active, causal and 'adult' voices of women, are themselves rarely in a position to define the 'field of recognition' – that is, children. And it is the ways in which their cognitive and imaginative perspectives are represented in theatre that the next section considers.

4 Feminist Practices of Care and Political Agencies of Children

Kasia Lech

The previous sections explored how female artists claimed agency over the narratives related to women, their circumstances, broader communities and their historical and sociopolitical contexts, diagnosing the past and present and proposing new solutions. Here, I move to explore how women artists in Poland empower the agency of others, specifically young children. The focus is on works aimed at and made with audiences below the age of ten and concerned with the politics of care and radical kinship understood as the need to prioritise the notion of 'co-existing in ways that ensure everyone's survival' (Ticktin in Woodly *et al.*, 2021, p. 921). The emphasis on '*everyone's* survival' is fuelled by various crises: the 2015 humanitarian-migration crisis, the global COVID pandemic, and, reappearing throughout this Element, the 2022 full escalation of the Russian invasion of Ukraine.

Patriarchalism conditions women's relation to care and children. In a Polish context patriarchalism is also politicised and sanctified through the Romantic paradigm and the Catholic Church imaginaries related to the 'Polish Mother' and Holy Mary (see Introduction). As previous sections have indicated, there are numerous examples of women and children brought together through acts of violence and the patriarchal lack-of-care. In a theatre context, there is also the issue of the low status accorded performances for young spectators. As art 'for children' and 'by women', theatre for young audiences has been traditionally positioned as less significant in sociocultural, political, artistical, and scholarly discourses (e.g. Klein, 2005; van de Water, 2012; Gardner, 2022; Chajbos-Walczak and Małkowicz, 2024).

In the theatre discussed in this section, the focus is on how women artists free the children-care-women nexus from these patriarchal associations: how care is reconceived so that young children from Poland, Ukraine, and Belarus might gain agency and imagine – and start creating – alternative ways of living and relating within and in-between societies. Hence, theatre for children becomes a source of what scholars describe as a transformative power arising from the ties between 'the fates and definitions of women and children' (Thorne, 1987, pp. 85–86), especially in the context of contesting relations of power, rethinking social relations and otherness (Osgood and Robinson, 2019, p. 2; Bodén and Joelsson, 2023, p. 482). Ultimately, within this remodelling of care, women, and children have a capacity to empower each other; political agencies are potentially activated in the interests of imagining more equal and hopeful futures.

4.1 'Pedagogika Teatralna': Politics and Practices of Care in Poland's Theatre

In the collection of short texts – framed as a critical exchange – on a new politics of care, Rachel Brown and Deva Woodly define it as 'a collection of principles, practices, and laws that facilitate communal gathering and the governance of polities'. These serve, they argue, as 'a gateway to but also preparation for a different kind of politics, one presenting us with new possibilities for living together' (Woodly *et al.*, 2021, pp. 894–895). The idea of new togetherness, as argued by Miriam Ticktin in the same collection, means 'co-existing in ways that ensure everyone's survival' and is underpinned by Audre Lorde's seeing care in relation to marginalisation as 'an act of political warfare' inherently related to survival (Lorde, 1988, p. 131; Woodly *et al.*, 2021, p. 916).

The genealogy of politics of care in Polish theatre has multiple (hi)storylines. Marzena Wiśniewska traces theatre's practices related to care, pedagogy and emancipation back to the 1920s, when Polish artists started writing about concepts such as theatre laboratory, improvisation, collaborative creation, and theatre-society relations (Wiśniewska, 2018). In terms of the development of current thoughts and practices, a significant moment came at the start of the twenty-first century when the term 'pedagogika teatru' (literally theatre pedagogy) appeared in Poland.[37] It was a translation of the German term 'theaterpädagogik.' Justyna Sobczyk pioneered it in Poland after graduating from the master's-level programme, Theaterpädagogik at the Universität der Künste in Berlin. The term 'pedagogika teatru,' says Wiśniewska, became 'the glue' for new ways of relation-building in Polish theatres at that time (2018, p. 16). The significance of the term was also connected to institutional support. In 2005, Sobczyk was hired at the newly formed Zbigniew Raszewski Theatre Institute (ZRTI) in Warsaw, which in 2015 opened a special department dedicated to the field.

'Pedagogika teatru' fuelled a systemic change, reimagining theatre-audience-society relations. The theatre workshops started by Sobczyk in the 2000s at the special education school in Warsaw developed into the Centrum Sztuki

---

[37] I will continue to use the Polish term *pedagogika teatru* rather translating it into English to emphasise the specifically situated practices it denotes in Polish context.

Włączającej / Teatr 21 (Centre of Inclusive Art / Theatre 21). It became an awarded with prizes and grants theatre institution with its building and an ensemble of actors primarily with Down syndrome and autism. This was unprecedented in the Polish theatre system which adhered to the idea of an actor with a 'perfect' and all-abled body. While this image still prevails, the artists of Theatre 21 now collaborate with Poland's leading theatre institutions.[38]

'Pedagogika teatru' is differentiated from the broad field of theatre or drama education – well established in Poland. It is rooted in a politics of care and imagining of togetherness. 'Pedagogika teatru' deploys a broad range of theatre practices embedded in changing sociocultural realities. Such practices use theatrical tools to facilitate a collaborative, creative, and multifocal reflection of reality with participants. Egalitarianism and emancipation are the guiding principles to create safe spaces where different views and experiences can meet and be in dialogue (Ogrodzka, 2016; Czarnota-Misztal and Szpak, 2018; Rochowska, 2019). As powerfully put by Dorota Ogrodzka – a researcher and practitioner of theatre – the essence of Polish 'pedagogika teatru' is 'the possibility of using the language of theatre to comment on, experience and interrogate theatre itself, or perhaps even more importantly, to interrogate, experience and create the [new] world' (2016). Bringing theatre together with the politics of care, 'pedagogika teatru' becomes a political practice of care.

In contemporary Polish theatre, the practice of care happens in various ways. Many public theatres have pedagogy departments that seek to engage with adult and young audiences. In the Jerzy Szaniawski Theatre in Wałbrzych, the theatre pedagogue Renata Ambrożak attends some performances wearing an armband with a cross resembling the Polish emergency room service. The idea is that a spectator can talk to her about the performance if they want to, immediately after the show or during the break. She 'administers' immediate care. In the Wrocław Puppetry Theatre, where Katarzyna Krajewska leads the pedagogy department, various workshops expand the productions' themes and support the young audience's agentic exploration. Other workshops invite children to play with theatre techniques. At the 2024 Przegląd Nowego Teatru dla Dzieci (New Theatre for Children Festival) organised by the theatre, seventeen shows were accompanied by thirty-three workshops, which provided a space for young people to voice and explore their responses to the performances.

---

[38] The work of Teatr 21 has been discussed in English by scholars such as Wiktoria Siedlecka-Dorosz (also a theatre pedagogue) and Sara Taylor (Taylor, 2018; Siedlecka-Dorosz, 2020).

The Stowarzyszenia Pedagogów Teatru (Association of Theatre Pedagogues) facilitates workshops exploring how to build a supportive and consensual environment in which culture is created in a way that takes care of various needs and challenges of those involved in the work. TR Warszawa invites children to play with theatre as their carers watch productions aimed at adult audiences. The theatre is now led by Anna Rochowska, a theatre pedagogue who replaced famous director Grzegorz Jarzyna. At the Współczesny Theatre in Szczecin, the pedagogy department led by Marta Gosecka offers, among other events, workshops for teachers to explore together how to engage young people in school with theatre productions they encounter.

The practices differ across the field, and individuals develop them. For example, Anna Kierkosz – the Educational and Project Curator from the Guliwer Puppet Theatre in Warsaw – developed an authorial practice that builds on socio-education, art pedagogy, and 'pedagogika teatralna' (Kierkosz, 2025).[39] Through this method, she leads a project #połączenia (#connections), where children work with theatre makers to explore and create new social bonds. I will circle back to Kierkosz's work; first I turn to the practices of Anna Wańtuch, which shift adult–child relations and present children's creative and political agency as a core element in debates about the future,

4.2 (Unpredictable) Children Reimagine Their Society: Anna Wańtuch and Families

Anna Wańtuch is a choreographer and pedagogue investigating relations between children and adults, whether mother-child, parent-child, or culture-child. Her practice is process-focused rather than production-led. The dramaturgies she develops have been discussed as led by change and unpredictability (Müller and Wycisk, 2022), which is emphasised by the presence of children who co-shape the work, and its porosity in a way that is not pre-set in rehearsal and can change in every performance. As Alicja Müller and Karolina Wycisk observe, the failures and disagreements between children and adults are an important part of the practice (2022) as visible in her work with Performujące Rodziny (Performing Families) rooted in the COVID-19 pandemic.

During the summer of 2020, Wańtuch invited families with children aged between one and half and five years – regardless of blood relations – for workshops to explore 'strategies for moving together, sharing individual and creative experience, building community choreography' (Wańtuch, 2020). The idea was to collaboratively create agentic and democratic methods for working

---

[39] For more, see 'Building Connections: Interview with Anna Kierkosz' at www.cambridge.org/Ewa.

together that also allowed each family member to develop and prepare a performance piece in which participants – whether performers or spectators – continued to feel agency and comfort to the extent that spectators also joined in (Czarnota-Misztal, 2021). This *Contact Families Show* was first presented online in December 2020, performed by adults and children. The young performers were between two and nine years old, an adjustment made in light of the children's ages in those families wanting to participate (Müller and Wycisk, 2022).

The online premiere happened because the workshops, although starting on-site, needed to move to Zoom because of the pandemic lockdown. Wańtuch reflected that while initially, the idea of creating closeness and participation through Zoom seemed pointless, the medium offered new possibilities for families to feel safe:

> First, I doubted whether it even made sense. It seemed absurd considering my core aims: closeness, relationship building, structures and geometry made up of small and large bodies. (...) Yet it turned out that my objectives spoke exactly to the needs of 'THIS time'. And suddenly, all the puzzles began to fit. The windows on Zoom quickly began to fulfil a need for equality and democracy, and the space of the house became comfortable and safe. The child could often go to the toilet independently and even unnoticed while the parent acted absorbed in improvisation. It was possible to make a sandwich with one hand and create a composition with toilet paper with the other. (Quoted in Czarnota-Misztal, 2021)

In other words, the project's initial aims – to reimagine being together as a family, as family participants, and as spectators – gained both urgency and strategies through the COVID-19 context. Through the project's commitment to dynamic change as a leading principle, the emergency and the new different methods of care and of being together – such as isolation – arising from the pandemic became incorporated into the project's practice of care. This, in turn, allowed for practices of everyday care and of public care (on stage) and of being together to get much closer, encouraging cross-pollination and making the everyday practices of play and of care and children's agencies culturally visible and sociopolitically important.

Justyna Czarnota-Misztal, describing the online premiere, said that at first, 'It looked like six families just fired up Zoom to meet each other and have a good time' (Czarnota-Misztal, 2021). In the first part, Wańtuch drew the names of choreographies which the families perform. These include exercises such as *drzewo* (tree: a child climbs on an adult), or *mikrostyki* (micro-contacts: contact through touching a minimal body part). In the second part, families performed pre-rehearsed improvisation. Crucially – as emphasised by Müller and Wycisk – children did not follow any strict choreographies. Instead, the movement was shaped by and shaped dynamic, trust-based relations between a child and their adult, enhanced through experiences from the process. The agency of the child was extra-present in the online context as they could easily choose when to be visible or invisible (by leaving the camera frame) (Müller and Wycisk, 2022).

At specific moments, the audience was encouraged to turn on cameras and join the movements. Slowly, says Czarnota-Misztal, the cameras of some spectators turned on, and people joined the movements. The audience included members of performing families that had not been in physical contact since the lockdown. Czarnota-Misztal specifically mentions a grandmother for whom joining her grandchildren's movements became a meaningful way of being with them during the pandemic (Czarnota-Misztal, 2021). This seemingly informal, intimate, and private form of performance nevertheless had public consequences. Müller and Wycisk highlight the radical political potential of 'unpredictable' children taking co-agency of how public space was structured and encountered, connecting it to queer practices and viewing it as 'speculations about possible, more inclusive futures' (Müller and Wycisk, 2022).

At the same time, there was also less speculative and more immediate impact as the structure developed in the project continued to be encountered by different communities. The *Contact Families Show* had an on-site premiere in the summer of 2021 during the Art Biennale for Children organised by the Centrum Sztuki Dziecka (Arts Centre for Children) in Poznań. This time, the event was expanded through new participants from Poznań who developed their version during the physical workshops – nevertheless informed by the methods created in the pandemic sessions – before the Biennale. Kraków and Poznań groups performed, and the project continued with different families.[40]

The practices created in the *Contact Families Show* evolved through the work of the Performujące Rodziny (Performing Families) company, which Wańtuch formed with children and their adult relations. One of their works is *Rośnie i rośnie* (*It's growing and growing . . .*), which premiered in Poznań in 2023. It focused on the future: on imagining growing up and getting older. Dressed in colourful loose clothing, carrying transparent balloons, and moving multicoloured blocks, families – including Wańtuch's own family – performed their versions of the future. For example, adults and children showed how they imagined their bodies getting older. The latter included both choreographies about how their bodies would relate to each other in future and the idea of children's bodies growing, aging, rendered by the children climbing on the adults. This climbing movement – both supportive and based on trust that the child would not hurt themselves or their adult – embodied Ticktin's core

---

[40] For the trailer see: www.youtube.com/watch?v=t8jzJfXx-kk.

principle of the politics of care: 'co-existing in ways that ensure everyone's survival' (Ticktin in Woodly *et al.*, 2021, p. 921).

Throughout *Rośnie i rośnie*, audiences were encouraged to become participants. The piece seemed like a finished production, but also a rehearsal. The children often broke into what appeared to be improvised and free play, and spectators tried out participation. But, in a larger sense, *Rośnie i rośnie* is a rehearsal for children, parents, and spectators growing older together as partners in family and society. Czarnota-Misztal again took an advisory role. This time, the role was formally named 'the care for the creative process', emphasising the multiple layers: care for family, care for children, care for on-stage partners (as per the climbing example), and the care in the process and for the process. Through all of this, care for everyone's well-being – in the broad sense – and the political agency of children (with its unpredictability) were presented as an inherent element for reimagining the future.

The works that Wańtuch co-created with children and adults and their emancipating potential were made in the context of Polish society. I will now turn to works for children in which the practices of care and the new relations they imagine have moved beyond geographical, cultural, and linguistic borders.

4.3 Collective Response-ability to and for the Vulnerable Other: *Yemaya–Królowa Mórz*

Yemaya–Królowa Mórz (*Yemaya–The Queen of Seas*) – aimed at audiences six years old and above – was written by Małgorzata Sikorska-Miszczuk and directed by Martyna Majewska for the Wrocław Puppet Theatre in 2016.[41] The immediate context for this production was the humanitarian crisis connected to the arrival of refugees – primarily from the Middle East – to Europe. Sikorska-Miszczuk explained that when she wrote the play, uppermost in her mind was the death of Alan Kurdî, a three-year-old Syrian boy who drowned in the Mediterranean Sea in September 2015 (Piekarska, 2016). The show received multiple praise and awards, including being the finalist of the prestigious 2017 National Competition for the Production of a Polish Contemporary Play.

In Poland, this humanitarian crisis was manipulated by the fearmongering tactics in the parliamentary election campaign by the Law and Justice Party (see Introduction). One of their key strategies was building on and enhancing anti-migrant and anti-Muslim fears in Poland. The public discourse and fear of 'other' were exemplified by the 2016 report which stated that the word 'refugee' was used by schoolchildren in Poland as an insult (Anannikova, 2016). In

---

[41] For the trailer see: www.youtube.com/watch?v=7P3UiA4zZ40.

March 2016 – *Yemaya* premiered at the end of May – Prime Minister Beata Szydło announced that Poland would not accept any refugees – including orphans – from Syria (despite the EU agreement signed by Poland). *Yemaya* was one of the first theatre works in Poland to directly address this issue.

The plot – set 'a long, long time ago ... or maybe not so long ago ... in fact, quite recently' as spectators were told at the start – centred around a five-year-old boy Omar (Agata Kucińska). He lived with his father (Igor Kujawski) – immediately challenging the patriarchal idea of the primary carer as a woman – in a beautiful white city that one day disappeared. Omar and his father embarked on a boat trip through a big sea. Curious about the sea, Omar leaned too far over the side of the boat and fell into the water. Under the sea, he met Queen Yemaya (Marta Kwiek) and multiple animals while his father waited for him on the shore.

The white city had no name, but the colour (also present in Anna Haudek's scenography) evoked associations with Aleppo and its destruction in the war in Syria since 2011. It was also difficult not to associate the big water with the Mediterranean Sea. At the same time, the show made no specific references to any places, languages, or wars. *Yemaya* was presented as a fable or allegory that could happen anywhere, and its core aim was to awaken Poland's/spectators' collective response-ability to and for vulnerable the Other. Some might call it a collective or national conscience, especially given that the show was narrated by the character named National Conscience (Jolanta Góralczyk), who remained stage-left throughout the entire piece. (Stage right was where Father-Kujawski stayed after Omar-Kucińska fell into the water.) Both Góralczyk and Kujawski remained just outside of the stage frame. At the same time, in the centre, Omar-Kucińska had a lot of fun underwater.

These two scenic spaces – one inside the main stage frame and one outside – were the spatial manifestations of two dramaturgies that independently guided audiences of adults and children to Omar, his father, and an alternative relationship with otherness. The main dramaturgy structured a story in which Omar encountered and played with multiple creatures, including Shark Gogo (Grzegorz Mazoń), who moved on Heelys shoes or rapping Dinosaur Molecule Hugo (Sławomir Przepiórka). These creatures sometimes spoke Polish – in *Yemaya* representing a human language that Omar could understand – and sometimes communicated through a made-up language (Hugo) or vocalisations (Yemaya). In other words, understanding each other's languages was presented as not essential to having fun together. This experience of playing with otherness was extended to children when Hugo-Przepiórka – in a made-up language – taught spectators to pronounce Omar's name. In other words, Hugo-Przepiórka's 'foreign' made Omar's 'foreignness' familiar. The otherness and not-understanding were at the same time presented not only as a base for an exciting play but also for learning about each other, in ways resonant with contemporary scholarship on connections between multilingualism, relation to otherness, and equality (e.g. Karpinski, 2015; Lech, 2024b).

As children built a relationship with Omar – with a hope that future Poland can respond differently to refugees – Majewska and Sikorska-Miszczuk used silence as a dramaturgical tool to invite adult spectators to imagine a relationship with otherness beyond the us-them framework of fear. National Conscience-Góralczyk and Father-Kujawski performed this dramaturgy. They both remained mostly silent (but visible) during the under-the-water events. Only in short moments of quietness on the main stage – for example, during a scene change – did spectators hear Father-Kujawski calling 'Omar, Omar'. These calls significantly impacted adult spectators. During the live performance I attended (in October 2016), the quiet sobbing of adults contrasted with children screaming and laughing as they played with Omar.

Kujawski's silence was simultaneously broken – as he called his son – and reinforced, when he was met with silence. Such silences can be understood as a parent's psychologically, neurologically, and biologically motivated need to keep a child safe (Bakermans-Kranenburg and van IJzendoorn, 2017; van 't Veer et al., 2019). This motivation was additionally emphasised in *Yemaya* by recognisable experiences of not seeing one's child, calling them, and hearing silence in response: on a playground, busy street, shop, airport, or a beach. Such silence is often filled with fear, anxiety, and worry, as the most common emotions when one's child goes missing (Nen et al., 2013, p. 17). In other words, the silences in *Yemaya* invited adult audiences to hear their fears in the silence of Kujawski (and in the silence he received when he called Omar) and, perhaps, for a moment, to see themselves in Father Kujawski. In turn, these silences worked against seeing the Other through the idea of stranger-danger, facilitated by Poland's public discourses at that time. The afore-discussed strategies allowed adult spectators to hear the sounds of collective response-ability to and for the vulnerable in the silence of Góralczyk as National Conscience. As Marta Bryś pointed out:

> After a performance like this, how could an adult tell their child that Omar and his dad might love the environment and are generally cool, but one should not help them find a new home? (Bryś, 2017)

Sikorska-Miszczuk and Majewska created *Yemaya* in Poland, which refused to care for the 'Other'. The production's relational and political potential resided in creating circumstances in which adults and children – together but independently – could imagine the possibility of encountering someone different to them in a way that was open-ended and not dictated by fear. It was created thinking about Poland, in which children had no first-hand war experiences. After Russia's full-scale invasion of Ukraine in February 2022, when children arriving in Poland had direct encounters with war, *Yemaya* was no longer performed, which was in itself an act of care.

In contrast to *Yemaya*, my final example arose from children's experiences of war, specifically displacement, but also recruitment of parents to the army and disruption of education (Lava *et al.*, 2022), and, on the other hand, the sense of welcoming 'strangers' into one's society. *Kosmiczny pokój* (*The Space Room/Peace*) was co-created by children for whom war shifted social and familial lives; together, they rehearsed and staged the political agency of children to imagine a future with peace and an appreciation for differences.

4.4 Rehearsing Alternative Ways of Living: *Kosmiczny pokój*

The title of *Kosmiczny pokój* (2023)[42] – a production for children aged five and above – by the Guliwer Puppet Theatre in Warsaw – played on the fact that the Polish word 'pokój' is a homonym. The noun denotes 'a room' (in a house, apartment, or a hotel) and 'peace' as either an antonym of war or a formal treaty ending a war. Thus, the title translates into English as *The Space Room* and *The Space Peace*. The double meaning underpinned the plot.

Kosmiczny pokój told the story of eight-year-old Emma, who lived in Warsaw with her mum while her dad remained in their country to fight in a war. As Emma spoke with a Ukrainian accent – she was performed as a three-actor animated puppet and led and voiced by Ukrainian Krystyna Velychko – one assumed that her father was in Ukraine and Emma is one of approximately 150,000 who, in September 2023, attended Polish education after arriving in Poland post-2022 Russia's full-scale invasion (Tędziagolska, Walczak and Wielecki, 2023). Their integration into the schools and their communities had been difficult. According to research commissioned by educational and children's rights organisations, some reasons included war and displacement-related stress and language, as Polish and Ukrainian are not mutually understandable. Poland's education system had little previous experience with migration. While general principles of diversity were promoted in schools, there were very few ideas on how to put them into practice in a way that respected and celebrated mutual differences. In turn, according to the reports, Ukrainian and Polish school children functioned in separate peer groups, and their interactions included xenophobic language and behaviours, and violence (Biuro Rzecznika Praw Dziecka, 2023; Tędziagolska, Walczak and Wielecki, 2023).

---

[42] For trailer see: www.youtube.com/watch?v=xyE39C-Cilc.

Kosmiczny pokój reflected these experiences. Emma-Velychko felt lonely and disliked by the children at her new school in Warsaw. After she was not invited to a birthday party, and she had no one to ask to come to her birthday party, she made a wish: 'I want peace in the world.' Simultaneously, her Polish school peer, Pola (a puppet led by Polish actor Izabela Zachowicz), also made the same wish. But its gravity was different. Pola made her wish during a beauty contest in which she participated to escape classes. She delivered an ironic speech in which she said that beauty contests promoted the idea that beauty was women's main contribution to society and were a waste of time and other valuable sociopolitical resources. However, she said, as an exemplary participant, she wished for world peace. The thoughtless ovation from the jury showed that her political agency as a young woman and a child was ignored.

Pola and Emma's wish(es) were heard by Wielkie Oko (Great Eye) (Damian Kamiński), which was the spirit of Emma's telescope. In *Kosmiczny pokój* (Figure 2), spirits from particular objects worked for Gwiazdka z Nieba (Star from the Sky/Heaven) (Izabella Kurażyńska), a Polish metaphor for the ultimate, best wish coming true. Oko-Kamiński only started their career and misunderstood pokój-as-peace for pokój-as-room, delivering 'pokój we wszechświecie' (a room in Space) instead of 'pokój na świecie' (peace in the world). As Emma and Pola tried to figure out their way back home, they were supported by strange, displaced objects: Niebieska Kanapa (Blue Couch) performed by Honorata Zajączkowska), Jednorożec (Unicorn), a toy played by Tomasz Kowol, and Kwiatek (Flour) enacted by Wojciech Parszewski.

Like Pola and Emma in the space, the objects were displaced – their stories connected to various movements of people, whether cross-border migration or a move to a house. Oko-Kamiński was also displaced but from a language. Performed as a non-gender character, Oko-Kamiński needed to break the grammatical rules of the deeply gendered Polish language to perform themselves. The difficult emotions – fear, sense of abandonment, sadness – were shown and validated through all those stories. At the same time, it was by building on these different and combined experiences that the two girls and the objects found their way back home and friendship. On the most basic level, this suggested that something positive could occur from something terrible. This was not to silver-line the tragedy of war but to offer hope. Moreover, by showing feelings, voices, and accents connected to displacement, the production stated that they contributed to Poland's culture. The production showed how solutions to communal problems could be addressed and resolved from the multifaceted perspectives of displacement and marginalisation. The intersectional marginalisation that the characters experienced because they were different – as queer, migrants, non-human, children, and women – was

Figure 2 A scene from 'Kosmiczny Pokój' (The Space Room/Peace) with Emma (Krystyna Velychko), Pola (Izabela Zachowicz), and Wielkie Oko (Great Eye) (Damian Kamiński). Photo by Marek Zimakiewicz.

therefore shown as an essential perspective to address problems encountered in society.

The experiences of otherness that *Kosmiczny pokój* staged also arose from the process underpinned by difference and multivocality. The piece was co-created by Magdalena Mrozińska (Polish writer), Kateryna Lukianenko (Ukrainian director), and Ukrainian, Polish, and Belarussian children aged seven to fourteen and living in Warsaw. After a long debate about the balance between the need to acknowledge their co-authorship and to protect their right to privacy (Kierkosz, 2025), they were named in the programme as Katia, Emma, Makary, Tetiana, Oleh, Nikita, Vika, Lilit, Tosia, Kamilek, Benio, Rita, Tymek, Hania, Zachary, Leo, and Basia. Approximately half of the group are refugee children.

Kosmiczny pokój was created in the summer of 2023 in interdisciplinary workshops co-facilitated by Mrozińska, Julianna Chrzanowska (a specialist on diversity and equality), Ukrainian actor Krystyna Velychko (who played Emma), (previously mentioned in this section) Anna Kierkosz, as *Kosmiczny pokój* happened in the context of her project #połączenia. The idea for the *Kosmiczny pokój* arose from children's different experiences of displacement (also from gender norms), their decision to create their own 'rooms' and one shared room in the workshop space, and pillow fights, which participants enjoyed. During such a fight, one of the Ukrainian children said: 'I would like a world with only pillow wars' (Kierkosz, 2025). The participants wrote two songs imagining such a world: Polish-language *Kolęda o pokoju* (*A Christmas Song about Peace/Room*) and multilingual *Piosenka o naszych marzeniach* (*A Song About Our Dreams*).[43] Based on these events and other ideas that emerged from the workshops, Mrozińska wrote the text, which children read performatively to the actors at the start of rehearsals. Throughout rehearsals, they were asked for feedback and contributed to the final production's dramaturgy, scenography, and choreography (Kierkosz, 2025).

The premiere was preceded by a press conference, which the young creators co-organised and co-led, speaking about the process, emphasising the production's theme and stressing the creative agencies that underpinned the making of the show (Kierkosz, 2025). However, they also framed the production as exemplifying how differences – shaped by the agencies of children, women, and migrants – could empower society, as evinced in those moments when Velychko as Emma asked children in the audience for help with Polish words, inviting them to rehearse what it might mean to host someone in their language.

This section engaged with processes and performances of different practices of care in theatre made by women artists for and with children, which allowed young people and adults to rehearse recognising, responding, and sharing response-ability for and to vulnerable others, and each other. Interrogating various intersectional marginalisations related to language, ethnicity, age, gender, displacement, and history, children and women were exploring and making arguments for the empowering and transformative potential arising from alliance-building. This potential was rooted in the opportunity to look at the reality around them from a new, multivocal perspective. From this, it was possible to gain a perspective on the present that, in turn, allowed for a more hopeful future. The potential of alliances to create the possibility of more hopeful futures is returned to in the following, final section of the Element.

5 Alliances and Realistic Cross-Border Utopias

Ewa Bal

Judith Butler, analysing the performative power of assemblies, pointed to the important relationship between the struggle for gender rights and the struggle for social justice:

> Gender politics must make alliances with other populations broadly characterized as precarious (Butler: 2015, p. 66) Alliances that have formed to

---

[43] *Kolęda o pokoju* (*A Christmas Song about Peace/Room*): www.youtube.com/watch?v=1w9x_xIf-Ls; *Piosenka o naszych marzeniach* (*A Song About Our Dreams*): www.youtube.com/watch?v=Ad_vulULd0s.

exercise the right of gender and sexual minorities must, in my view, form links, however difficult, with the diversity of their own population and all the links that implies with other populations subjected to conditions of induced precarity (...) crossing communities of language and cultural formations. (Butler, 2015, p. 67)

Alliances understood in this way answer a central question posed in this Element: What connects the issues of fighting patriarchy and rape culture in war-torn Ukraine, with the reclaiming of women's gendered history and reproductive rights in Poland? This is because the projects developed by alliances of Ukrainian and Polish women theatre makers, which I will discuss in this section, form a specific feminist imagination and epistemology located in Central and Eastern Europe.

The issue of reclaiming women's reproductive rights in Poland, as we indicated in the introduction, has intensified over the last decade, both in public debate and in the theatre. It has been accompanied by a growing awareness in Polish society of the oppressive legacy of the Catholic Church, which, as Marcin Kościelniak has suggested, after the period of systemic transformation in Poland enjoyed unlimited influence on current state policy, including the creation of the legal order and reduction of women's role in society to that of mothers and homemakers (Kościelniak, 2024, p. 23). It is, therefore, not surprising that the criticism of this institution found expression in the numerous theatre projects that Polish women artists carried out, first independently and later in collaboration with Ukrainian artists.

5.1 Ukrainian-Polish Theatre

From the very beginning, however, it was possible to see that this critique was intersectional, as it also involved the LGBTQ+ community, which understood the oppressive influence of the church, if only because of the lack of the right to enter into civil unions. As Polish theatre critic Aneta Kyzioł writes, these productions 'serve to reflect not only on the state of the Church itself, but above all on the state of the society shaped by this institution and in its shadow. This society is ready to crucify or to passively watch the crucifixion, but unable to see its neighbour in the crucified and to empathise with his pain' (Kyzioł, 2022, p. 76). There were productions such as *Klątwa* (*The Curse*), directed by Olivier Firlič at the Powszechny Theatre in Warsaw, in which, in the final scene, one of the actresses cut down a cross with a saw as a sign of disapproval for the contempt shown to women who have unwanted pregnancies. Jakub Skrzywanek, a representative of the gay community in Poland, in his production *Śmierc Jana Pawła Drugiego* (*The Death of John Paul II*) in 2020 at the Polish Theatre in Poznań, presented a re-enactment of the last hours of Karol Wojtyła's life. Instead of his iconic figure, cemented in memory by the media, the audience assisted to the re-enactment of a dying process of an old, coughing, and frail man.

At the Powszechny Theatre in Warsaw, Agnieszka Błonska directed *Diabły* (*Devils*, 2019), in which Oksana Cherkashyna, like Sinead O'Connor in former times, accusingly holds in her hands and then half-gifts a photograph of Archbishop Marek Jędraszewski. The latter has uttered hateful phrases about the LGBTQ+ community, calling it an 'ideology'. Criticism of the Church's influence was also evident in *Spartakus. Miłość w czasach zarazy* (*Spartacus. Love in Times of Cholera*, 2022), directed by Jakub Skrzywanek at the Współczesny Theatre in Szczecin, which focused on children and adolescents who end up in closed, psychiatric wards as a result of previous suicide attempts and depression caused by peer bullying and homophobia (Karpinska, 2022). Finally, like politically engaged performances in Latin America (Taylor, 2016), theatre in Poland has taken on the role of celebrating those ceremonies that the state deems illegal. For example, it performs weddings for same-sex couples on stage in place of a church, hostile to such weddings (with which, in Poland, the state has signed a concordat).[44]

This critical face of Polish theatre and its open political commitment attracted Ukrainian artists from the 'self-made' generation, who were looking for an appropriate theatrical language to express their own bodily experiences: the violence of patriarchy, rape culture, the disciplining of gender and sexuality inherited from Soviet times, or sexual harassment in cultural institutions. The highly criticised position of the director-master in Poland, who abuses his power over actresses, was met with similar criticism of the school of psychological acting and the all-powerful director in Ukraine (Harbuzyuk 2023b). The common goals of female artists from Poland and Ukraine resulted in projects that were realised in both countries. The best examples of such cooperation were the initiatives of Joanna Wichowska on the Polish side and representatives of the Ukrainian theatre community, among others: Roza Sarkisian, Oksana Cherkashyna and the NGO 'Theatrical Platform' led by Iryna Chuzhynova. Two projects were realised in this format: *Mapy strachu mapy tożsamości* (*Maps of Fear – Maps of Identity*, 2016) and *Mij did' kopal, mij bat'ko kopal, a ja ne bydu* (*My Grandfather Used to Dig, My Father used to dig, and I won't*, 2018) in different Ukrainian cities (Kyiv, Lviv, Mariupol). In Poland, there were

---

[44] Here I refer to the 'weddings' performed on stage for same-sex couples at the end of the play *Spartacus. Love in the Time of Cholera* directed by Jakub Skrzywanek, or the 'Ukrainian Wedding' by actress Oksana Cherkashyna and Zoya Laktionova, which took place on the stage of the Powszechny Theatre in Warsaw, with the participation of the local LGBTQ+ community.

two editions of the festival *Bliscy Nieznajomi – Ukraina* (*Close Strangers-Ukraine*, 2020), *Bliscy Nieznajomi – Wschód* (*Close Strangers – the East*), 2021, organised by Agata Siwiak and Joanna Wichowska at the Polski Theatre in Poznań, which brought together not only Polish-Ukrainian productions but also a local queer community.

Wichowska developed the method of devised dramaturgy in Ukraine and entered into a critical dialogue with cultural norms, manifestations of nationalism, models of national suffering, and patriarchy, and openly criticised Poland's colonial view of Ukraine. On the other hand, Ukrainian female directors such as Roza Sarkisian and Olena Apchel (currently fighting on the Ukrainian front) have been working in Poland, where they directed a series of theatre productions with strong political, anti-Catholic overtones. There have been many Ukrainian artists working simultaneously in the two countries, such as playwrights: Katerina Penkova (known for her sharp texts criticising sexual harassment in the education system and the management of Ukrainian theatres) or Lena Lagushonkova (who mercilessly criticises the patriarchal, nationalist, and pro-Russian face of eastern Ukraine).

This Polish-Ukrainian collaboration resulted in theatrical projects that propose 'apotropaic (salvific) narratives' or 'realistic utopias' on stage (Domańska, 2021). Building on Jameson's idea of utopia (Jameson, 2005, p. 416, 2010), feminist standpoint theory (Braidotti, 2014) and concepts of epistemic (in) justice (Mignolo, 2011, p. 277, Santos, 2014, p. 42), Domańska asserts:

> realistic utopias that I am trying to instigate here (and that is also evident in the fields of ecological or environmental humanities and in scholarship on the Anthropocene) creates, I believe, a space for producing a particular form of knowledge – knowledge that is built 'in spite of the times' and filled with the ideals of an affirmative ethics and politics – as well as an equally sceptical approach to the tendencies that are emerging in the reactionary politics of fear, negativism, impending apocalypse, overpowering trauma, shortage, emptiness, weak subjectivity, and passive victims … Such utopias are governed by a principle of prefiguration that is based on creativity, imagination, and experiments in innovative practices.… I am turning toward realistic micro-utopias that can be realized on temporally and spatially limited local scales – that is, they operate in specific times and for the needs of particular communities (by improving community members' well-being). (Domańska, 2021, p. 152)

I devote the following part of my discussion to the analysis of such salvific utopias of the future, that have been created within the framework of Polish-Ukrainian alliances, by analysing (1) the performances of *Dziady* (*The Forefathers' Eve*, 2021), directed by Maja Kleczewska from the Juliusz

Słowacki Theatre in Kraków and *Dziady* (*The Forefathers' Eve*, 2023), also directed by her, for the National Drama Theatre in Ivano-Frankivsk (Ukraine), (2) *Kreszany* (*The Trees' Spirit*, 2021), directed by the Ukrainian artist Olena Apchel from the Zagłębie Theatre in Sosnowiec/Poland, and (3) *Radio Mariia* (2022) from the Powszechny Theatre in Warsaw by a Polish-Ukrainian team: director Roza Sarkisian (Ukraine), playwriters Joanna Wichowska and Krysia Bednarek (Poland).

5.2 Subverting National Mythologies

One way in which Polish feminists reformulated national mythologies, as previous sections have shown, was through a critical or openly speculative reading of Polish Romantic literature. The latter established a historiosophical sense of Poland's existence and assigned social roles to the sexes in accordance with the Catholic worldview. It is therefore not surprising that the Polish director Maja Kleczewska, famous for her feminist and political interpretations of the classical repertoire, decided to take a thoroughly critical look at the iconic Polish cultural drama *Dziady* (*Forefathers' Eve*) (Figure 3).[45] She cast an actress (Dominika Bednarczyk) in the male lead role of the poet Konrad. In the prison cell of the Basilian Church in Vilnius, instead of the former anti-Tsarist Polish conspirators of the nineteenth century, there are actresses playing Polish activists, participants in the aforementioned pro-choice movement Women's Strike. Significantly, they bear clear traces of blood on their faces, a reminder of the aggressive police interventions against them during street demonstrations. Kleczewska showed them sitting in a cell, watched by CCTV cameras, the images of which we also saw on a large screen stretched across the stage. By this she wanted to emphasise that it is women who are the driving force in Polish society, even if their starting position is precarious.

When full-scale war broke out between Russia and Ukraine, Kleczewska added to her production a prologue from Adam Mickiewicz's poem *Do Przyjaciół Moskali* (*To My Friends the Muscovites*), in which accusatory words are uttered against the Russians: 'Perhaps one of you, disgraced by his office, disgraced by his order,/ has forever given his free soul to the grace of the Tsar,/ and today worships him at his doorstep.'[46] This text was performed by an Ukrainian actress, signalling that the fate of Ukraine, left alone by Europe in the fight against Russians, resonated in this production with the voice of women in Poland betrayed by their own state. The remedy for this betrayal was to be the

---

[45] For the trailer see: https://youtu.be/ar6rTT2gl14.
[46] https://wolnelektury.pl/katalog/lektura/dziady-dziadow-czesci-iii-ustep-do-przyjaciol-moskali.html.

Figure 3 A scene from 'Dziady' (The Forefathers' Eve) with Priest Piotr (Marcin Kalisz) and Ewa (Karolina Kazoń). Photo by Bartek Barczyk for the Juliusz Słowacki Theatre in Kraków.

central monologue of the drama *Dziady*, called 'Improvisation', originally attributed to the male character. However, the Polish actress Dominika Bednarczyk transformed it into a feminist utopia. With her tender, hushed voice, she sketched a vision of a new, better world based on empathy and affect. This power of affect, the press wrote, 'breaks through in the singer's perfectly pitched and confident voice – in that power that will "roll down and lift up thrones" if only it could finally break through the human throat . . . ' (Feldberg, 2021).

However, in this production, more important than the typical feminist 'reclaiming of the voice' seems to me to be the way in which the director has dealt with the Polish Church. In the prayer scene, Father Piotr (the same priest who in the original drama saved Konrad from blasphemy by performing an exorcism on him) is standing in front of the altar, which in the theatre faithfully imitates the sculptures of the late Gothic Church of St Mary in Krakow. The priest is suddenly disturbed by the presence of a young girl – Eve (who in the drama was the lover of the poet Konrad). Without further ado, the priest rapes her right in front of the historical altar, which for the audience is clear evidence of the Church's violence against women (and children) and its guilt for the contemporary shape of legislation in Poland. Of course, Kleczewska has radically simplified the interpretation of this drama, but precisely in order to make it clear, through an ostentatious gesture, that the existing patterns of national culture, built with the support of the Catholic Church (with its obsession with power, misogyny, paedophilia and moral corruption) – must be destroyed. Destroyed in the same way that the feudal world order and the power of the Russian Tsar had to be destroyed in the nineteenth century.

The intersectionality of the Polish-Ukrainian alliance, this time formed directly against Russia as the common enemy, is demonstrated by the fact that a few months after Russia's full-scale attack on Ukraine, when Ukrainian people were still fleeing their country, Maja Kleczewska made quite an arduous decision, to stage *Dziady* also for Ukrainian audiences in Ivano-Frankivsk, in the west of the country.[47]

For this purpose, she retained the spatial scenographic solutions of her Krakow production, such as a prison cell set into a trap door from which surveillance cameras showed the conspirators. She did, however, modify the anti-Church message by replacing the Catholic priest Piotrr with the Russian Orthodox Patriarch Kirill, who actively supported Putin in the war against Ukraine. She also changed the interpretive direction of Mickiewicz's drama – returning, as it were, to its original anti-Russian message. And in the prison cell, instead of nineteenth-century Polish conspirators (and instead of women, as in the Polish production), there were actors playing Ukrainian soldiers, the heroic defenders of Azovstal, whom the Russians tortured in captivity, many of whom have still not returned to their homes.

Kleczewska also restored the decidedly patriarchal overtones of Mickiewicz's work, showing that today's Ukraine – which found itself in exactly the same position as Poland at the end of the eighteenth century, when it fell victim to the Russian Empire, or when it was attacked by Russia in 1939 – requires manly generosity. These historical parallels between the fates of Poland and Ukraine were important for the director and for the Polish audience who later saw the performance.

The political and interventionist nature of the performance, however, was only revealed in the so-called 'Salon Scene' (in the original it was set in the court of the tsar's governor, Novosilcov, in Warsaw). In Kleczewska's staging, it alluded to the awards ceremony at the Cannes Film Festival, when in 2022 a naked activist appeared with the Ukrainian flag painted on her body and the words 'Stop raping us'. It was also a gesture of protest against the lack of empathy of Western European societies and the lack of understanding about the Ukrainian 'cause', since Russian film director Kirill Serebrnikov was invited to the festival. Kleczewska recreated the atmosphere of the Cannes red carpet in the theatre and cast an actress playing the mother of a soldier held captive by the

---

[47] For the trailer see: www.youtube.com/watch?v=WcukOPxUdWs.

Russians (Ms Rollinson) in the role of an activist. With this arrangement, the director linked, by analogy, several different historical times and places: contemporary Europe, unable to free itself from the colonial grace of Russian culture; the war in Ukraine; and the age-old struggles of Central and Eastern Europe against Russian imperialism, as well as the precarious position of women in all these times and places.

This openness to different times and historical contexts of the Ukrainian production was evident during the performances at the 2023 'Divine Comedy Festival' in Krakow, when a Polish actress, the Polish Konrad of our time (Dominika Bednarczyk), shared the stage for a moment with the Ukrainian Konrad (played by Roman Lutsky). The message that the fight for social justice requires alliances across borders and gender was clear to the Polish audience. Kleczewska though has not completely abandoned the romantic patriarchal paradigm of the heroic struggle. From a feminist point of view, it would probably have been better if the alliance on stage had been between women. Nevertheless, it was a culturally and historically significant gesture, bringing the two nations, Polish and Ukrainian, closer together after years of hostility and alienation.

5.3 New Mythologies and Epistemologies from the East

Ukrainian director Olena Apchel went much further than Kleczewska in dismantling the Judeo-Greco-Christian cultural heritage on the basis of the national mythologies that underpin it.[48] I refer to her production *Kreszany* (*The Threes' Spirit*s, 2021) (Figure 4) staged in the Zagłębie Theatre in Sosnowiec (Poland).[49] The script was written by Olena Apchel, in collaboration with Olha Matsiupa (Ukraine) and Wojtkek Zrałek-Kossakowski (Poland).

The performance is framed by Ukrainian girls in military uniforms, played by Polish actresses, sitting in the trenches in Donbas during the war that has been going on there since 2014. They talk about the unwillingness of their army to accept women in it. There is a lack of everything: uniforms, shoes, no one even thinks of providing sanitary pads for women. However, their conversation is only a pretext to start a play in which other possible utopian worlds are imagined as alternatives to the European historiosophical imaginary of war. Following the challenge of decolonial scholars who have called for the unlearning of Western European epistemology (Mignolo and Tlostanova, 2012) and the

---

[48] 'Kreszany' were Slavic goddesses with the body of a bird who guarded the Tree of Fiery Apples. This tree emerged from the chaos of the cosmos and was the source of the knowledge of good and evil (24.03.2022).

[49] For the trailer see: www.youtube.com/watch?v=R7pGQ43lo2w and www.youtube.com/watch?v=CskmXOmC6os.

Feminist Imagining in Theatres 59

Figure 4 A scene from 'Kreszany' (The Threes' Spirits). Group Scene. In the centre there is a rock statue of Baba, a female figure from the Donbas region of Ukraine. Photo by Pawel Wojciechowski.

'provincialisation of Europe' (Chakrabarty, 2007, pp. 3–23), Apchel's main concern is to get Europeans to admit their ignorance or unlearn their thinking habits for once. In her production, the figure of knowing/un-knowing is epitomised by a replica of an ancient stone statue of a 'baba', one of many that can still be found around Dnipro in eastern Ukraine (the director's own hometown) and that have survived almost intact for more than six thousand years.[50]

The Ukrainian term 'baba', according to etymologists, is derived from a Persian root meaning 'warrior',[51] which can be interpreted as a brave version of femininity. However, there are so many ideas about the origin of both the word 'baba' itself and the Dnipro statues and their function that it is better to speak of an accompanying 'not knowing' rather than of scientific certainties. These mysterious totemic statues of unknown genealogy are, on the one hand, mute witnesses to centuries of pre-Christian history and, at the same time, their enigmatic nature makes us aware of the limits of human knowledge. In Apchel's production, based on the structural principle of speculative 'what if' thinking (Gallagher, 2017), the stone Baba points to the need to move the western

---

[50] https://vesti.dp.ua/legendarni-skifski-babi-dnipra-vidkrivayut-sekreti-foto/, (24.03.2022).
[51] https://znaj.ua/history/183812-spadshchina-pradavnogo-narodu-yaku-tayemnicyu-prihovuyut-unikalni-kam-yani-babi-dnipra (24.03.2022).

epistemic perspective to the East (eastward). At the same time, it encourages us to find an alternative founding myth of European culture, by saying:

> I have stood here in the steppe for hundreds of years, billions of mushrooms have spawned new colonies on me, some six and a half million pigeons have shat on me, dozens of empires have been born and died before my eyes. And I still stand – Baba me, Baba stone me – with my face to the east.[52]

This is why, in the next scene, on a large screen the audience watches a stylised old black and white mockumentary recording of a hypothetical conversation between the first Polanian prince Mieszko I (baptised in 966 by Emperor Otto III) and Olga of Kiev (baptised in 957 in Constantinople and responsible for the Christianisation of Kiev Rus at the cost of the slaughter of the Slavic Drevlani who opposed Christianity), and Olga's grandson, Vladimir I the Great, who continued to consolidate Orthodoxy in Kyiv Rus. These figures look at their work of Christianisation from a contemporary perspective and apparently doubt the success of their mission. Olga Kyiv emphasises that Christianity has reduced the role of woman to that of guardian of the hearth and mother, depriving her of social agency, and in these observations she is echoed by both Mieszko I and Vladimir.

However, the most interesting challenge, in my view, that the play's creators pose to a Western epistemology based on Greek-Judeo-Christian mythology is to invite spectators to look at the character of Clitajmestra from the perspective of feminist concerns. This challenge sounds similar to the one once formulated by Judith Butler (2010) for Western culture to listen more closely to the voice of Antigone, who, in accordance with the law of kinship and in defiance of the patriarchal law enacted by Creon, wanted to bury her brother. Like Butler, Olena Apchel would like us to see Clitajmestra as the wounded mother of Iphigenia, whose life her father sacrificed on the altar of war to ensure the success of his mission, instead of Agamemnon's murderess. Her plea was, therefore, very topical at a time when the whole world has seen that the innocent victims of the war taking place are the women and their children who are being raped by the Russian invaders.

Therefore, the most important moment in this play is Clitajmestra's monologue, which is a proposal of speculative and decolonial thinking. By combining

---

[52] Olena Apchel, Olha Matsiupa, Wojciech Zrałek-Kossakowski, *KRESZANY* albo JAK PTAKI NA DRZEWIE AWOKADO ŚWIAT TWORZYŁY, A MECH I KOPALINY TĘ WIEŚĆ ROZNOSIŁY Spotkanie z echem słowiańskiego liberalnego matriarchatu w postsłowiańskim świecie kryzysu Europy nie tylko środkowej* (KRESZANY* or HOW THE BIRDS ON THE AVOCADO TREE CREATED THE WORLD, and the mosses and the fossils spread the message, encountering the echoes of Slavic liberal matriarchy in the post-Slavic world of crisis, not only in Central Europe), a manuscript in PDF file, thanks to Wojciech Zrałek-Kossakowski.

Slavic and Greek mythology, Clitajmestra emphasises the importance of matrilineal cultural heritage. She wants to give birth to Iphigenia again, but this time not in the cradle of Western Greek culture (where she will inevitably die at the hands of her own father), but in the East. She also wants to replace the misguided Erynes (the former goddess of vengeance), who had forgiven Orestes' murder of his mother and who, along with Apollo, helped to legitimise a democracy based on patriarchy, with the Slavic goddesses of birth and rebirth – the Rodzanice [Parentheticals]

The scene culminates in Iphigenia's poetic monologue to her mother, Clitajmestra, which is also Olena Apchel's own confession to her mother, who died in the Donbass. In it, she expresses her longing for the organic land (now occupied by the Russians), for the smell and taste of kasha eaten in the old days, for the warmth of home, and for that which – as the accounts of many people displaced against their will show – gives us a sense of belonging to a broader community:

> Every spring. I remember carrying six cucumbers in my hands to exchange with my friend Ola for a loaf of bread. Where her mother worked, wages were paid in bread, and for your work, you got a bit of porridge, barley porridge, I think. For many years I hated barley porridge. I am that porridge. Created from its particles. From the details of the porridge. The grains cooked in the mucus that surrounds them. (...) The atom from the cell on the skin of my right wrist was once the atom in the eye socket of the first reptile to emerge from the ocean into the desert. (Apchel, 2021, Kreszany)

The attachment to ancient flavours, home and land is formulated in a discourse that refers to the cellular structure of living beings as well as to the atoms of matter. This discourse testifies to the fact that, at the most material, molecular level, our bodies and those of our ancestors and the geological strata of the earth belong to a common system based on reciprocal relationships, as Karen Barad (2007) and Jane Bennett (2010) have written extensively. Theatrical performance, moreover, activates in the spectator what decolonial scholars have called 'co-feeling-thinking' ('sentir pensar', 'corazonar', 'feeling-thinking', Taylor, 2020, Santos, B. de S., 2018, Bal, 2021). Indeed, the platform for this encounter was 'vibrant matter', as Bennett put it, or 'slough media' (Schneider, 2020), that is, an organic site of decomposition and growth, a place where different geological layers come into contact with each other. Slough media become a vehicle for a peculiar archaeology of knowledge, enabling relations with deeper layers of time and matter, which are accessed precisely through the compassionate thinking activated by art.

From this materialist-empirical and, at the same time, affective perspective, the ritual of communion, typical of the Christian religion, can look quite different, as the creators suggest. For it can be imagined as an act of transmitting life on a molecular level. The difference is that instead of the male body of Christ, typical of the Western world, the Slavic goddess Rodzanica (Parenthetica), the mother of the daughter, plays the role of the consumed wafer in this act of devotion.

Such a replacement of the male body of the god (Christ) with the female body of the goddess (or, as one actress put it, the replacement of the belief in a 'god on a stick' with the belief in a 'goddess body') would certainly have far-reaching cultural consequences. Starting with the fact that the typical patriarchal concept of bravery and bloody sacrifice in defence of the values of civilizational progress and the nation would have to be replaced by the concept of caring for loved ones and so-called 'significant others' (Haraway, 2003), who may represent the values of longevity or self-renewing socionature (De La Cadena, 2015, p. 8). In *Kreszany*, therefore, it becomes clear to the viewer that there is an intuitive desire to combine the aspirations of feminist indigenous scholars from overseas with those of a feminist philosophy grounded in the Central-Eastern European experience. Thus, intersectionality and alliances are to be understood not only as a joint struggle for gender rights, but also precisely as a post-anthropocentric transcending of the human perspective.

5.4 From Mythologies to Social Practice

While Olena Apchel proposes to reformulate Greek-Judeo-Christian cultural heritage through Slavic mythology and to reconsider the role of non-human subjects in our culture, Roza Sarkisian and Joanna Wichowska, in their production *Radio Mariia* (2022) from the Powszechny Theatre in Warsaw, propose to move away from religion altogether towards concrete social solutions.[53] Their play, set in the editorial office of 'Radio Mariia', whose name derisively mocks the well-known Polish Catholic ultra-right radio station 'Radio Maryja', is an example of speculative, utopian thinking about the future as an accomplished present.

It begins in 2037, the fifteenth anniversary of the collapse of the Catholic Church in Poland. Events familiar to the viewer in 2022 – such as women protesting in the streets to regain their reproductive rights, the impossibility of same-sex unions and, finally, the widespread presence of the Church in public life – are now only a memory of a bygone era of social inequality. The Jubilee radio programme begins by celebrating the moment of the Catholic Church's demise in the form of a short performance by a radio editor, played by Oksana Cherkashyna. The editor, dressed as the Virgin Mary, claims to be the

---

[53] Images from the productions are available at: www.powszechny.com/en/spektakle/radio-mariia.

embodiment of all the artists who have criticised the Catholic Church in their art. She then adds:

> I am not divine, I am not a mother,
> I had an abortion in the costume of Our Lady Queen of Poland.
> On the stage of the Powszechny Theatre,
> on a small stage, I aborted Jesus and all his images.

She then took off her costume of the Virgin Mary and threw it into a large dustbin, along with all the ecclesiastical attributes lying on the floor: chasubles, chalices, crosses, and holy images. Then, parodying the words of another Polish actress, Joanna Szczepkowska, who said on television on 4 June 1989: 'Ladies and gentlemen, on 4 June 1989 communism ended in Poland,' Cherkashyna said: 'Ladies and gentlemen, 15 years ago the Catholic Church ended in Poland'. This gesture, both physical and verbal, of the end of an era is significant insofar as, according to the interpretation proposed in this Element, real political transformation, both in Poland and in Ukraine, will not take place without a thorough demolition of its rotten foundations, namely the privileged position of the Church and the 'old power of the patriarchy'.

This is why the show, which unfolds to the rhythm of the radio programme, occasionally invites guest speakers to share their observations on the world before and after the feminist revolution. Invited by the editor, the well-known Polish activist and feminist sociologist Elżbieta Korolczyk or the creator, performer, and queer activist Magdalena Staroszczyk discusses in all seriousness how the intersectional demands postulated in the previous sections of this Element have found their practical form in the new feminist reality. And the reality in Poland in 2037, as they describe it, looks extremely optimistic.

The times when feminists fought against the Church are merely the subject of entertainment by reconstruction groups (like a football match between a team of priests and a team of women). Money from property confiscated from the Church has been used to build public transport lines linking every town in Poland. Church buildings were converted into homes for people in crisis. Elzbieta Korolczuk also explains that the radical upheaval occurred when women protesters were joined by all sections of society, including women in the church structures, under the slogan 'Nuns to the barricades'. A broad social movement, the queer community, representatives of capital, the police, and the doctors themselves took part in this in order to fundamentally reform health services and transportation.

In this show, utopia is seen as a realistic, needs-based solution to improve social and individual life, in which religion no longer plays a role: neither as a worldview, nor as a ritual, nor as a discipline, nor as a community.

According to the playwrights, community is built through specific actions for the benefit of others, distributed equally among all members of society: for example, care work is shared equally among men, women, trans, and non-binary people.

However, in place of religion, other rituals of celebration have emerged, such as dancing and singing, and a secular cult of the uninhibited body: 'vaginatism' or 'hexism' or sex with plants. There is, of course, no shortage of humour, as when the editor announces that the remnants of the Catholic Church, led by Bishop Jędraszewski, have managed to flee Poland for Russia, but that the relevant services are already looking for and pursuing them. For, as Oksana Cherkashyna warns, there is no such thing as a revolution once and for all, and the women's war goes on and on.

And this is both a positive and a disturbing summary of my reflections thus far. For on the one hand, in the theatre projects discussed here, the desire for social change seems visible and legible, in the spirit of a truly post-social and intersectional solidarity capable of overthrowing regimes (even regimes as powerful as tsarism, communism or the church used to be), and transcending national borders as well as species and gender divisions. On the other hand, it is essential to be aware of the fragility of the goals achieved through intense social and cultural efforts given the conservative turn currently unfolding in many European countries and the United States, with the active and passive support of Russia. This makes it all the more important to listen to the voices of women theatre artists from Central and Eastern Europe, whose situated experiences 'speak' to and assist ongoing feminist struggles for a more hopeful future.

6 Final Reflections

Kasia Lech and Ewa Bal

In this jointly authored Element, we brought together two feminist epistemological perspectives from Ukraine and Poland. We explored their differences and, in turn, looked to the shared, intersectional vision emerging from works by women theatre artists from both countries. The starting point was our conviction that (1) there were analogous patriarchal imaginaries of femininity in the two countries that derived from the shared violent histories, experiences of colonialism, including Poland towards Ukraine, Russia towards Ukraine and Poland, and the two countries' colonial subordination to the Soviet Empire;[54] and (2) these patriarchal imaginaries and their historical underpinnings affected hostilities between Poland and Ukraine. The politicised images of women as caring

---

[54] For more on the relationship between Soviet and Russian colonialism and imperialism see Thompson (2000).

mothers, crucified sufferers, objectified youth, and silent victims of violence we identified as present in the dramatic literature, theatre, and iconography of both countries. Such images have been persistently transmitted through culture almost to the present day. They embody patriarchal fantasies associated with an ethos of systemic transformation which dominant public perceptions in Ukraine and Poland, as well as in the international arena, posit as the achievement and the victory of brave men.

In contrast, the Element focused on how women theatre artists in both countries interrogated and sought to transform the oppressive patriarchal structures inherent in their national cultural imaginaries, proposing new solutions based on alliances and realistic utopias that offered new insights into both the past and the future. While the works we analysed differed in style, themes, contexts, and audiences, they were always rooted in the struggle for subjectivity, human rights, survival, justice, and for radical, feminist epistemic change on national and international levels. This, together with the growing awareness of mutual differences and, at the same time, connectedness through intersectional marginalisations affecting women from the region, both locally and as 'Eastern Europeans', led to the formation of artistic alliances.

The Element discussed the processes, practices, and motivations of women's theatre making in four contexts. In Section 2, the focus was on Polish women's efforts to recover herstories and defy invisibility, oppression, and objectification rooted in national histories and collective memories related to the 1989 transformation. Section 3 analysed the agency of theatre in Ukraine during war time, and showed how performance can transform the effects of hate speech and rape culture into a strategy of resistance, one that involves partisan guerrilla tactics in the face of a much stronger opponent. Section 4 highlighted how the transnational alliances between women and children freed the child-care-woman nexus from patriarchal associations and empowered their respective political agencies to envision more equal and hopeful futures. Section 5 developed the concept of imagined feminist futurities based on Polish-Ukrainian intersectional alliances both in the theatre productions and in social engagement, proposing alternative national and transnational mythologies and radical, social changes.

The 'feminist imaginings' by women theatre artists from Poland and Ukraine that emerge in the Element denote diversely situated processes of looking from the East, and, simultaneously, problematise dichotomies related to Europe's East and West and mutual imaginaries arising from them. The political potential and urgency of such imaginings extend beyond the interrogation and reimagining of immediate contexts. For instance, the discussion of Ukrainian and Polish women *together* takes Ukraine out of the discourse on Russia and the former USSR, re-positioning Ukrainian and Polish women's subjectivities within new perspectives that break established stereotypes and imaginaries. Equally, exploring the histories of Ukraine and Poland from transnational and feminist perspectives also takes Poland out of the role of 'eternal victim', showing historical power structures from a different angle, and dismantling discourses that construct Russia as always dominant in the region and as its 'natural' ruler. Hence, the voices of women artists from Poland and Ukraine problematise overly simplistic and fixed ideas about colonisers and the colonised, offering crucial and significantly underexplored perspectives on decolonisation and global justice. In sum, it is not only the 'feminist imaginings' of the artists that are uncovered throughout this Element, but also the way in which their theatre connects and contributes to a reassessment of the geopolitics of knowledge.

References

Ahmed, S. (2012) *On Being Included: Racism and Diversity in Institutional Life*. Durham: Duke University Press.

Anannikova, L. (2016) 'Mówią: Nie chcemy ich, niech lepiej zginą', *Gazeta Wyborcza*, 12 December.

Bakermans-Kranenburg, M. J. and van IJzendoorn, M. H. (2017) 'Protective Parenting: Neurobiological and Behavioral Dimensions', *Current Opinion in Psychology*, 15, pp. 45–49.

Bal, E. (2021) 'Od poddaństwa do poznawczej suwerenności. Perspektywy badań współczesnych praktyk wiedzo-twórczych kultur lokalnych', *Didaskalia*, 166.

Bal, E. (2023a) 'Cracking the Field of Linguistic Recognition on the Cultural Mobility of Ukrainian Drama in Poland after 24 February 2022', *Pamietnik Teatralny* 72, pp. 81–98.

Bal, E. (2023b) 'Słodko śpiąca Europa albo trzy spektakle o wojnie', *Didaskalia*, 177.

Bal, E. (2024a) '*Fucking Truffaut*. O wojnie w teatrze idiotycznym', *Didaskalia*, 179.

Bal, E. (2024b) 'Ukrainian Gambit. Postcolonial Perspectives on the First Shakespeare Theatre Festival in Ukraine', *Critical Stages*, 30.

Bal, E. and Chaberski, M. (2021) 'Introduction: Situated Knowing: From Performance Art to the Laboratory of Knowledge-Making', in E. Bal and M. Chaberski (eds) *Situated Knowing Epistemic Perspectives on Performance*. London: Routledge, pp. 1–7.

Barad, K. (2007) *Meeting the Universe Halfway*. Durham: Duke University Press.

Bennett, J. (2010) *Vibrant Matter: A Political Ecology of Things*. Durham: Duke University Press.

Biuro Rzecznika Praw Dziecka (2023) *Sytuacja dzieci i młodzieży z Ukrainy w polskich szkołach*. Warszawa: Biuro Rzecznika Praw Dziecka.

Bodén, L. and Joelsson, T. (2023) 'Advancing Feminist Relationality in Childhood Studies', *Childhood*, 30(4), pp. 471–486.

Borger, J. (2022) 'Russia Is Guilty of Inciting Genocide in Ukraine, Expert Report Concludes', *Guardian*, 27 May.

Braidotti, R. (2014) 'Conclusion: The Residual Spirituality in Critical Theory: A Case for Affirmative Postsecular Politics', in R. Braidotti, B. Blaagaard, T. de Graauw, and E. Midden (eds) *Transformations of Religion and the Public Sphere: Postsecular Public*. Basingstoke: Palgrave, pp. 249–272.

References

Bryś, M. (2017) *Omar – chłopiec taki jak ty, Encyklopedia Teatru Polskiego.* https://encyklopediateatru.pl/artykuly/238531/omar-chlopiec-taki-jak-ty (Accessed: 7 January 2025).

Butler, J. (1997). *Excitable Speech: A Politics of the Performative.* London: Routledge.

Butler, J. (2010a). *Frames of War: When Is Life Grievable?* London: Verso.

Butler, J. (2010b). *Antigone's Claim: Kinship between Life and Death.* New York: Columbia University Press.

Butler, J. (2011). *Bodies That Matter: On the Discursive Limits of Sex.* London: Routledge.

Butler, J. (2015). *Notes toward a Performative Theory of Assembly.* Cambridge, MA: Harvard University Press.

Cervinkova, H. (2012) 'Postcolonialism, Postsocialism and the Anthropology of East-Central Europe', *Journal of Postcolonial Writing*, 48(2), pp. 155–163. https://doi.org/10.1080/17449855.2012.658246.

Chajbos-Walczak, K. and Małkowicz, Z. (2024) *Badanie środowiska osób zajmujących się sztukami performatywnymi i literaturą dla dzieci i młodzieży.* Poznań: Centrum Sztuki Dziecka.

Chakrabarty, D. (2007) *Provincializing Europe: Postcolonial Thought and Historical Difference.* Princetown: Princetown University Press.

Chuzhynova, I. (2025) 'Скандал в університеті Карпенка-Карого: чи є шанс зупинити некроз системи', *Українська правда*, 28 January.

Crenshaw, K. (1989) 'Demarginalizing the Intersection of Race and Sex: A Black Feminist Critique of Antidiscrimination Doctrine, Feminist Theory and Antiracist Politics', *The University of Chicago Legal Forum*, 140, pp. 139–167.

Czarnota-Misztal, J. (2021) 'Strategie na bliskość', *Dialog*, (7–8), pp. 230–242.

Czarnota-Misztal, J. and Szpak, M. (2018) 'Wstęp', in J. Czarnota-Misztal and M. Szpak (eds) *Pedagogika teatru. Kierunki, refleksje, perspektywy.* Warszawa: Instytut Teatralny im. Zbigniewa Raszewskiego, pp. 4–7.

De la Cadena, M. (2015) *Earth Beings: Ecologies of Practice across Andean Worlds.* Durham: Duke University Press.

Díez-Bedmar, M. del C. (2022) 'Feminism, Intersectionality, and Gender Category: Essential Contributions for Historical Thinking Development', *Frontiers in Education*, 7. Available at: https://doi.org/10.3389/feduc.2022.842580.

Domańska, E. (2021). 'Prefigurative Humanities', *History and Theory*, 60(4), pp. 141–158.

Fábián, K., Johnson, J. E. and Lazda, M. (2021) *The Routledge Handbook of Gender in Central-Eastern Europe and Eurasia, the Routledge Handbook of Gender in Central-Eastern Europe and Eurasia.* London: Routledge.

Feldberg, K. (2021) 'Ciemności kryją ziemię i lud we śnie leży. Wokół spektaklu *Dziady* w reżyserii Mai Kleczewskiej w Teatrze im. Słowackiego w Krakowie', *Kultura Liberalna*, 675(50).

Fidelis, M. (2010) *Women, Communism, and Industrialization in Postwar Poland*. Cambridge: Cambridge University Press.

Fidelis, M., Kirin, R. J., Massino, J., and Oates-Indruchova, L. (2014) 'Gendering the Cold War in the Region: An Email Conversation between Malgorzata (Gosia) Fidelis, Renata Jambrešić Kirin, Jill Massino, and Libora Oates-Indruchova', *Aspasia*, 8(1), pp. 162–190.

Fischer-Lichte, E. (2008) *The Transformative Power of Performance: A New Aesthetics*. London: Routledge.

Gallagher, C. (2017) *Telling It Like It Wasn't, Telling It Like It Wasn't*. Chicago: University of Chicago Press.

Gardner, L. (2022) 'Theatre Professionals who Devalue Kids' Theatre Need to Grow up', *The Stage*, 14 February.

Ghabra, H. and Calafell, B. M. (2018) 'From Failure and Allyship to Feminist Solidarities: Negotiating Our Privileges and Oppressions across Borders', *Text and Performance Quarterly*, 38(1–2), pp. 38–54.

Glajar, V. and Radulescu, D. (2005) *Vampirettes, Wretches, and Amazons: Western Representations of East European Women*. New York: Columbia University Press.

Glinianowicz, K. (2014) 'Czarnobrewe i czarnoziemy. O szlacheckim pożądaniu kolonialnym Ukrainy', *Miscellanea Posttotalitariana Wratislaviensia*, (2), pp. 161–173.

Górska, P. (2019) *Polaryzacja polityczna w Polsce. Jak bardzo jesteśmy podzieleni?* Warszawa: Centrum Badań nad Uprzedzeniami.

Graff, A. (1999) 'Patriarchat po seksmisji', *Gazeta Wyborcza*, 19 June.

Graff, A. (2014a) 'Gdzie jesteś, polski feminizmie? Pochwała sporu i niejasności', *Krytyka Polityczna*, 12 June.

Graff, A. (2014b) *Matka Feministka*. Warszawa: Krytyka Polityczna.

Graff, A. (2024) 'Pora przestać się dziwić', in M. Kościelniak (ed) *Aborcja i demokracja*. Warszawa: Krytyka Polityczna, pp. 8–18.

Habermas, J. (2022) 'War and Indignation: The West's Red Line Dilemma', *ResetDOC*, 14 October.

Haraway, D. (1988) 'Situated Knowledges: The Science Question in Feminism and the Privilege of Partial Perspective', *Feminist Studies*, 14(3), pp. 575–599.

Haraway, D. (2003) *The Companion Species Manifesto: Dogs, People, and Significant Otherness*. Chicago: The University of Chicago Press.

Harbuzyuk, M. (2023a) 'Overcoming Silence', *Critical Stages*, 28. https://www.critical-stages.org/28/overcoming-silence/.

Harbuzyuk, M. (2023b) '"We Could Have Ventured in the Opposite Direction." Exploring the Legacy of Polish Theatre on the Festival Map of Independent Ukraine', *Pamietnik Teatralny*, 72, pp. 57–80.

Hrycak, A. (2001) 'The Dilemmas of Civic Revival: Ukrainian Women since Independence', *Journal of Ukrainian Studies*, 26(1–2), pp. 135–158.

Huigen, S. and Kołodziejczyk, D. (eds) (2023) *East Central Europe between the Colonial and the Postcolonial in the Twentieth Century*. Cham: Springer International.

Hundorova, T. (2014) 'Postorientalizm, romans imigrancki nowe możliwości studiów postkolonialnych w Europie Wschodniej: Zarys dziejów traktora po ukraińsku Mariny Lewyckiej', *Miscellanea Posttotalitariana Wratislaviensia*, (2), pp. 87–106.

Jameson, F. (2005) *Archaeologies of the Future: The Desire Called Utopia and Other Science*. London: Verso.

Jameson, F. (2010) 'Utopia as Method, or the Uses of the Future', in M. D. Gordin, H. Tilley, and G. Prakash (eds) *Utopia/Dystopia*. Princeton: Princeton University Press, pp. 21–44.

Janion, M. (2006) *Niesamowita Słowiańszczyzna: fantazmaty literatury*. Kraków: Wydawnictwo Literackie.

Janoszka, M. (2014) '"Beniowski" we krwi: o kilku wymiarach symboliki "cieczy osobliwej" w poemacie Juliusza Słowackiego', in M. Piechota, M. Kalarus, and O. Kalarus (eds) *Granice romantyzmu: romantyzm bez granic?* Katowice: Wydawnictwo Uniwersytetu Śląskiego, pp. 100–115.

Karpińska, A. (2022) 'Oskarżamy i wyzwalamy', *Teatrdlawszystkich.com*, 29 November, https://teatrdlawszystkich.eu/oskarzamy-i-wyzwalamy (Accessed: 9 January 2025).

Karpinski, E. C. (2015) 'Can Multilingualism Be a Radical Force in Contemporary Canadian Theatre? Exploring the Option of Non-Translation', *Theatre Research in Canada/Recherches théâtrales au Canada*, 38(2), pp. 153–167.

Kasińska-Metryka, A. and Pałka-Suchojad, K. (2024) *Women in Eastern European Post-Socialist Countries Social, Scientific, and Political Lives*. London: Routledge.

Kierkosz, A. (2025) 'Personal Conversation with Kasia Lech on 21st January 2025'.

Klein, J. (2005) 'From Children's Perspectives: A Model of Aesthetic Processing in Theatre', *Journal of Aesthetic Education*, 39(4), pp. 40–57.

Korek, J. (ed.) (2007) *From Sovietology to Postcoloniality: Poland and Ukraine from a Postcolonial Perspective*. Huddinge: Södertörns högskola.

Kościelniak, M. (2018) 'Krucjata moralna Solidarność', *Teksty Drugie*, 5, pp. 25–44.

Kościelniak, M. (2024) *Aborcja i demokracja*. Warszawa: Krytyka Polityczna.

Kosiński, D. (2010) *Teatra polskie: historie*. Warszawa: Wydawnictwo Naukowe PWN.

Krings, T., Moriarty, E., and Wickham, J. (2013) *New Mobilities in Europe: Polish Migration to Ireland Post-2004*. Manchester: Manchester University Press.

Kuefler, M. (2024) 'The History of the History of Sexuality', in M. E. Wiesner-Hanks and M. Kuefler (eds) *The Cambridge World History of Sexualities*. Cambridge: Cambridge University Press, pp. 1–22.

Kułakowska, K. and Łuksza, A. (2015) 'Feminine Voice in Poland', *Feminist Media Studies*, 15(1), pp. 53–73.

Kwaśniewska, M. (2021) '#MeToo in Polish Theatre Education', *Facta Universitatis, Series: Philosophy, Sociology, Psychology and History*, p. 219.

Kyzioł, A. (2022) 'Klątwa Dziadów. O grzechach Kościoła w polskim teatrze', *Polityka*, August, p. 76.

Lava, S. A. G. et al. (2022) 'Please Stop the Russian-Ukrainian War – Children Will Be More than Grateful', *European Journal of Pediatrics*, 181(6), pp. 2183–2185.

Lease, B. (2016) *After '89: Polish Theatre and the Political*. Manchester: Manchester University Press.

Lech, K. (2024a) '"1989": wielogłosowość infranarracji a pamięć zbiorowa o polskiej walce o wolność', *Didaskalia*, 177.

Lech, K. (2024b) *Multilingual Dramaturgies: Towards New European Theatre*. Cham: Palgrave Macmillan. https://doi.org/10.1007/978-3-031-40624-9.

Lorde, A. (1988) *A Burst of Light: Essays*. Ithaca: Firebrand Books.

Maciejewski, Ł. (2005) 'Byłem Isaurą. "Niewolnica Isaura", czyli stan wojenny w telewizji', in W. Godzic (ed) *30 najważniejszych programów telewizji polskiej*. Warszawa: Wydawnictwo Trio, pp. 159–171.

Matusiak, A. (2020) *Wyjść z milczenia. Dekolonialne zmagania kultury i literatury ukraińskiej XXI wieku z traumą posttotalitarną*. Wrocław: Kolegium Europy Wschodniej im. Jana Nowaka-Jeziorańskiego.

McIntosh, M. D. and Hobson, K. (2013) 'Reflexive Engagement: A White (Queer) Women's Performance of Failures and Alliance Possibilities', *Liminalities: A Journal of Performance Studies*, 9(4), pp. 1–23.

Mickiewicz, A. (2003). *Dziady: część trzecia* (M. Adamiec, Ed.). Uniwersytet Gdański.

Mignolo, W. D. (2011) 'Geopolitics of Sensing and Knowing: On (de)coloniality, Border Thinking and Epistemic Disobedience', *Postcolonial Studies*, 14, pp. 273–283. doi:10.1080/13688790.2011.613105.

Mignolo, W. D. and Tlostanova, M. (2012) *Learning to Unlearn: Decolonial Reflections from Eurasia and the Americas*. Columbus: Ohio State University Press.

Mintz, S. (2008) 'Reflections on Age as a Category of Historical Analysis', *The Journal of the History of Childhood and Youth*, 1(1), pp. 91–94.

Miszczynski, M. and Helbig, A. (2017) 'Introduction', in A. N. Helbig and M. Miszczynski (eds) *Hip Hop at Europe's Edge: Music, Agency, and Social Change*. Bloomington: Indiana University Press, pp. 1–8.

Müller, A. and Wycisk, K. (2022) 'Miękkie choreografie. O tańcu eksperymentalnym dla rodzin', *Didaskalia*, 167.

Napiórkowski, M., Szyngiera, K. and Wlekły, M. (2023) '1989', *Dialog*, 797(4), pp. 73–133.

Napiórkowski, M., Szyngiera, K. and Wlekły, M. (2024) *1989. Pozytywny mit*. Kraków.

Nen, S., Alavi, K., Ibrahim, F., Mohd Hoesni, S., and Sarnon, N. (2013) 'Missing Children and Parental Struggle: From Chaos to Coping', *Pertanika Journal of Social Sciences and Humanities*, pp. 17–29.

Ogrodzka, D. (2016) 'Odsłaniając rusztowanie. Pedagogika Teatru czyli poszerzanie pola gry', *Dialog*, (4).

Okólski, M. and Salt, J. (2014) 'Polish Emigration to the UK after 2004; Why Did So Many Come?', *Central and Eastern European Migration Review*, 3(2), pp. 11–37.

Osgood, J. and Robinson, K. H. (2019) 'Introduction: Throwing the Baby out with the Bathwater? Traces and Generative Connections between Feminist Post-structuralism and Feminist New Materialism in Childhood Studies', in J. Osgood and K. H. Robinson (eds) *Feminists Researching Gendered Childhoods: Generative Entanglements*. London: Bloomsbury, pp. 1–16.

Ostrowska, E. (2004) 'Matki Polki i ich synowie. Kilka uwag o genezie obrazów kobiecości i męskości w kulturze polskiej', in M. Radkiewicz (ed) *Gender: Konteksty*. Kraków: Rabid, pp. 215–227.

Pascall, G. and Kwak, A. (2005) *Gender Regimes in Transition in Central and Eastern Europe*. Bristol: Bristol University Press.

Penn, S. (1994) 'The National Secret', *Journal of Women's History*, 5(3), pp. 55–69.

Penn, S. (2005). *Solidarity's Secret: The Women Who Defeated Communism in Poland*. Ann Arbor: University of Michigan Press.

Piekarska, M. (2016) '4. Przegląd Nowego Teatru dla Dzieci', *Gazeta Wyborcza*, 25 May.

Rochowska, A. (2019) 'Pedagogika teatru – próba definicji Zwrot edukacyjny w teatrze', *Kultura Współczesna*, 105(2), pp. 133–144.

Ruszkowski, P., Przestalski, A. and Maranowski, P. (2020) *Polaryzacja światopoglądowa społeczeństwa polskiego a klasy i warstwy społeczne*. Warszawa: Collegium Civitas.

Santos, B. de S. (2015) *Epistemologies of the South, Epistemologies of the South*. Routledge. doi:10.4324/9781315634876.

Santos, B. de S. (2018) *The End of the Cognitive Empire, the End of the Cognitive Empire*. Durham: Duke University Press.

Schneider, R. (2011) *Performing Remains: Art and War in Times of Theatrical Reenactment*. London: Routledge.

Schneider, R. (2020) 'Slough Media', in E. Bal and M. Chaberski (eds) *Situated Knowing Epistemic Perspectives on Performance*. London: Routledge, pp. 15–43.

Scott, J. W. (1988) *Gender and the Politics of History, Gender and the Politics of History*. New York: Columbia University Press.

Siedlecka-Dorosz, W. (2020) '"… And We All": The Phenomenon of Theatre 21', in K. Ojrzyńska and M. Wieczorek (eds) *Disability and Dissensus: Strategies of Disability Representation and Inclusion in Contemporary Culture*. Leiden: BRILL, pp. 200–214.

Slavova, K. and Stoilova, R. (2024) 'Intersectionality: Perspectives from Central and Eastern Europe', in K. Davis and H. Lutz (eds) *The Routledge International Handbook of Intersectionality Studies*. London: Routledge, pp. 28–41.

Sribna, T. (2011) 'Transformacja systemów politycznych Polski i Ukrainy: charakterystyka porównawcza głównych tendencji', *Środkowoeuropejskie Studia Polityczne*, (3), pp. 17–25.

Strokata, N. (1980) *Ukrainian Women in the Soviet Union: Documented persecution*. Baltimore: Smoloskyp Publishers.

Szwed, A. (2015) *Ta druga. Obraz kobiety w nauczaniu Kościoła rzymskokatolickiego i w świadomości księży*. Kraków: Nomos.

Szyngiera, K. (2023) 'European Theatre Forum 2023', in *Roundtable Artistic Impulse – Democracy, Collaboration, and the Power of Theatre*. Opole.

Taylor, D. (2016) *Performance*. Durham: Duke University Press.

Taylor, D. (2020) *¡Presente!* Durham: Duke University Press.

Taylor, S. (2018) 'When It's Written on Your Face: Teatr 21 and the Paradox of Invisibility', *TheTheatreTimes.com*, 23 March. https://thetheatretimes.com/written-face-teatr-21-paradox-invisibility/ (Accessed: 9 January 2025).

Tędziagolska, M., Walczak, B. and Wielecki, K. M. (2023) *Refugee Students in Polish Schools*. Warszawa: Centrum Edukacji Obywatelskiej. https://ceo.org.pl/udostepniamy-raport-uczniowie-uchodzczy-w-polskich-szkolach/ (Accessed: 9 January 2025).

Thompson, E. M. (2000) *Imperial Knowledge: Russian Literature and Colonialism*. London: Bloomsbury.

Thorne, B. (1987) 'Re-visioning Women and Social Change: Where Are the Children?', *Gender & Society*, 1(1), 85–109.

Ukraine. A different Angle on Neighbourhood (2021) Kraków: Międzynarodowe Centrum Kultury.

van 't Veer, A. E., Thijssen, S., Witteman, J., van IJzendoorn, M. H., and Bakermans-Kranenburg, M. J. (2019) 'Exploring the Neural Basis for Paternal Protection: An Investigation of the Neural Response to Infants in Danger', *Social Cognitive and Affective Neuroscience*, 14(4), pp. 447–457.

van de Water, M. (2012) *Theatre, Youth, and Culture, Theatre, Youth, and Culture*. Basingstoke: Palgrave Macmillan.

Wałęsa, D. (2011) *Marzenia i Tajemnice*. Warszawa: Wydawnictwo Literackie.

Wańtuch, A. (2020) *Anna Wańtuch i Performujące Rodziny, Facebook*. www.facebook.com/p/Anna-Wa%C5%84tuch-i-Performuj%C4%85ce-Rodziny-100063674435958/ (Accessed: 2 January 2025).

Wejbert Wąsiewicz, E. (2015) 'Współczesny teatr polski wobec aborcji.', *Kultura Popularna*, 44(2), pp. 82–95.

Wiesner-Hanks, M. E. (2015) 'Gender and Sexuality', in J. H. Bentley, S. Subrahmanyam, and M. E. Wiesner-Hanks (eds) *The Cambridge World History*. Cambridge University Press, pp. 133–156.

Wiśniewska, M. (2018) 'W stronę polskiego modelu pedagogiki teatru', in J. Czarnota-Misztal and M. Szpak (eds) *Pedagogika teatru. Kierunki, refleksje, perspektywy*. Warszawa: Instytut Teatralny im. Zbigniewa Raszewskiego, pp. 15–30.

Woodly, D., Brown, R. H., Marin, M., et al. (2021) 'The Politics of Care', *Contemporary Political Theory*, 20(4), pp. 890–925.

Żarnowska, A. (2004) 'Women's Political Participation in Inter-War Poland: Opportunities and Limitations', *Women's History Review*, 13(1), pp. 57–68.

Zychowicz, J. (2020) *Superfluous Women: Art, Feminism, and Revolution in Twenty-First-Century Ukraine*. Toronto: University of Toronto Press.

Acknowledgements

We are beyond grateful to Ukrainian research colleagues: the late Maia Harbuzyuk, Yana Partola, Iryna Chuzhynova, for their valuable comments and guidance. Thank you to Elaine Aston and Melissa Shira – the editors of Women Theatre Makers Cambridge Elements – for trusting us and sharing their knowledge with us through feedback and guidance. This Element was partly inspired by Elin Diamond, who in 2022 first asked us the question: what links Polish and Ukrainian feminism? The answer this question was underpinned by conversations with Olena Apchel, Roza Sarkisian, Agata Siwiak, Joanna Wichowska, Tamara Trunova, Oksana Dmitriieva, Natalka Vorozhbyt, Olga Matsiupa, Liuba Ilnytska, Oksana Cherkashyna, Nina Zakhozhenko, Lena Lagushonkova, Kateryna Penkova, Marta Keil, Monika Kwaśniewska, Katarzyna Krajewska, Anna Kierkosz, Magda Szpecht as well as Olha Baybak, organiser of the Premia Gra Festival (Ukraine). This book would not have been possible without the financial support of the Excellence Initiative Fund of the Jagiellonian University, and without women who taught us feminism, you know who you are.

Cambridge Elements

Women Theatre Makers

Elaine Aston
Lancaster University

Elaine Aston is internationally acclaimed for her feminism and theatre research. Her monographs include *Caryl Churchill* (1997); *Feminism and Theatre* (1995); *Feminist Theatre Practice* (1999); *Feminist Views on the English Stage* (2003); and *Restaging Feminisms* (2020). She has served as Senior Editor of Theatre Research International (2010–12) and President of the International Federation for Theatre Research (2019–23).

Melissa Sihra
Trinity College Dublin

Melissa Sihra is Associate Professor in Drama and Theatre Studies at Trinity College Dublin. She is author of *Marina Carr: Pastures of the Unknown* (2018) and editor of *Women in Irish Drama: A Century of Authorship and Representation* (2007). She was President of the Irish Society for Theatre Research (2011–15) and is currently researching a feminist historiography of the Irish playwright and co-founder of the Abbey Theatre, Lady Augusta Gregory.

Advisory Board

Nobuko Anan, *Kansai University, Japan*
Awo Mana Asiedu, *University of Ghana*
Ana Bernstein, *UNIRIO, Brazil*
Elin Diamond, *Rutgers, USA*
Bishnupriya Dutt, *JNU, India*
Penny Farfan, *University of Calgary, Canada*
Lesley Ferris, *Ohio State University, USA*
Lisa FitzPatrick, *University of Ulster, Northern Ireland*
Lynette Goddard, *Royal Holloway, University of London, UK*
Sarah Gorman, *Roehampton University, UK*
Aoife Monks, *Queen Mary, London University, UK*
Kim Solga, *Western University, Canada*
Denise Varney, *University of Melbourne, Australia*

About the Series

This innovative, inclusive series showcases women-identifying theatre makers from around the world. Expansive in chronological and geographical scope, the series encompasses practitioners from the late nineteenth century onwards and addresses a global, comprehensive range of creatives – from playwrights and performers to directors and designers.

Cambridge Elements

Women Theatre Makers

Elements in the Series

Maya Rao and Indian Feminist Theatre
Bishnupriya Dutt

Xin Fengxia and the Transformation of China's Ping Opera
Siyuan Liu

Emma Rice's Feminist Acts of Love
Lisa Peck

Women Making Shakespeare in the Twenty-First Century
Kim Solga

Clean Break Theatre Company
Caoimhe McAvinchey, Sarah Bartley, Deborah Dean and Anne-marie Greene

#WakingTheFeminists and the Data-Driven Revolution in Irish Theatre
Claire Keogh

The Theatre of Louise Lowe
Miriam Haughton

Ellen Terry, Shakespeare, and Suffrage in Australia and New Zealand
Kate Flaherty

Performing Female Intimacy in Japan's Takarazuka Revue
Nobuko Anan

Feminist Imagining in Polish and Ukrainian Theatres
Ewa Bal and Kasia Lech

A full series listing is available at: www.cambridge.org/EWTM

Printed by Integrated Books International,
United States of America